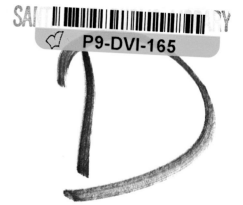

Your practical guide to
– HOME, GARDEN, FOOD, BEAUTY, MIND, WORK & PLAY –

The NEW ART *of* LIVING GREEN

How to Reduce Your Carbon Footprint and Live a Happier, More Eco-Friendly Life

ERICA PALMCRANTZ AZIZ & SUSANNE HOVENÄS

Photography and Graphic design by
BIANCA BRANDON-COX

Translated by
CHRISTEL PALMCRANTZ GARRICK

Skyhorse Publishing

Copyright ©2014 by Erica Palmcrantz Aziz and Susanne Hovenäs
Photography ©2014 by Bianca Brandon-Cox
Illustration ©2014 by Saga Aziz

Skyhorse Publishing books may be purchased in bulk at special discounts for sales promotion, corporate gifts, fund-raising, or educational purposes. Special editions can also be created to specifications. For details, contact the Special Sales Department, Skyhorse Publishing, 307 West 36th Street, 11th Floor, New York, NY 10018 or info@skyhorsepublishing.com.

Skyhorse® and Skyhorse Publishing® are registered trademarks of Skyhorse Publishing, Inc. ®, a Delaware corporation.

www.skyhorsepublishing.com

10 9 8 7 6 5 4 3 2 1

Library of Congress Cataloging-in-Publication Data is available on file.

ISBN: 978-1-62873-739-4

Printed in China

WHO WE ARE

Erica Palmcrantz Aziz

AGE: 36
FAMILY: Husband Sam and daughter, Saga
I LIVE IN: Gothenburg, Sweden, Planet Earth
I WORK: To inspire people to eat and live more with raw food. You should use this powerful tool, food, to live in a deeper connection with yourself, and be grateful for whatever there is. Raw food is a lifestyle where you make better choices for yourself, your brothers and sisters, and for this magical planet.
I DREAM OF: Every heart achieving the serenity of love, peace, and acceptance. Peace on earth begins in your own heart.
MY VISION: I hope to live more in, from, and around Nature. I want to grow and eat my own food, drink spring water, and walk barefoot everyday.

SUSANNE ABOUT ERICA: She is an amazing woman with total honesty and lots of love, who makes others feel fabulous. Few people have as much wisdom as this woman possesses.

Susanne Hovenäs

AGE: 44
FAMILY: Husband Håkan and two daughters, Nanna and Nelly
I LIVE IN: Stockholm, Sweden, Planet Earth
I WORK AS: A journalist and editor of one of the largest health magazines in Sweden, whose basic message is that by eating good food, getting a move on, and taking care of Nature, we feel better and may heal ourselves from diseases.
I DREAM OF: Moving closer to nature and using my words to continue to inspire others to discover the value of shifting the focus from the brain to the heart and see that everything is connected.
MY VISION: I hope to become more aware and accepting of things being just as they should be. I try not to judge without seeing the possibilities in each moment, and keep doing the best I can for Mother Earth.

ERICA ABOUT SUSANNE: She is a wonderful woman, bursting with energy and sharing life in a beautiful and generous way. Mrs. Inspiration is her middle name!

WHAT IS HAPPENING TO THE WORLD?

- Climate change and global warming
- Melting polar ice caps
- Ever more poisons on land and in oceans
- Bees facing extinction
- Chemical cocktails
- Biodiversity seriously threatened
- 30 percent of arable land more or less useless
- Increasing contamination of potable water sources
- Oceans becoming more acidic
- Devastation of rainforests
- Depletion of resources like oil, metals, phosphor, forests, etc
- Rising food prices
- Social unrest
- Financial crises

How fares our Mother Earth?

The symbiosis of Man and Earth

We are part of Nature and can not defy its laws. Man is part of the ecosystem where plants and animals live in the balance of a constant cycle.

An ecosystem is based in symbiosis—coexistence—where all parts are necessary. Everything hangs together in one great whole.

During the last hundred years man has upset the balance of all ecosystems in a remarkable way. Soon we will reach the so called 'tipping point,' that critical point of no return as far as the world climate is concerned. That is when the really catastrophic changes will become inevitable. But let's not despair; together we can help prevent 'tipping points.'

Environmental problems

Environmental problems are steadily increasing in spite of more active and organized eco-movements than ever before. An internationally skewed agricultural policy subsidizes those growers who use fertilizers and herbicides with enormous sums, even though this is harmful and has far reaching negative effects for both humans and the earth. Mother Earth is the basis for our existence and she reacts strongly to what is happening. Algae bloom, coral death, and the abnormally high number of hurricanes are only a few signs that the natural ecological system is in extreme imbalance. The ozone layer is alarmingly thinner and the greenhouse effect has brought long periods of rain and, for that matter, draughts, floods, and other natural catastrophes around the world. Clean water and clean air are scarce in many places. During the last forty years half of the freshwater reserves have been depleted and in twenty-five years they will be halved again.

FROGS IN HOT WATER

Our situation may be likened to what is called the frog-effect. When a frog is placed in a jar with cold water that is slowly heated, the frog remains. It gradually gets used to the rising temperature until it is finally cooked. But if you drop a frog into boiling water it would jump out at once. We are just like the frogs—we adjust and get used to it, but who wants to be boiled?

beeurban.se

Bees—crucial to our future

Did you know that every third bite of food you eat is pollinated by a honey bee? During the last decade it has been reported that the honey bee is unfortunately facing extinction and without bees our human existence is in jeopardy. We simply depend on the bees and bumblebees to fly around and help pollinate the plants. The genetic modification of plants is part of this threat to the bees.

Genetically modified organisms (GMOs) are plants that are created by biotechnology to be resistant to biocides—but can still carry various pesticides that harm bees and other insects.

It has not been proven that genetically modified vegetables and grains are hurting people directly, but it may lead to the death of the bees. Critics maintain that it is not sufficiently researched yet if GMOs are affecting humans.

What *is* happening is that bees flying freely find nectar containing pesticide two miles away from their hive. Thus the bees themselves may cause the spread of biocides from GMO-crops to crops that are not genetically modified.

The environment reflects our health

The environment and our lifestyle are direct reflections of how our Mother Earth really feels. Many people today are not in touch with themselves and instead of seeing our own uniqueness we try copying others.

In the western world anonymity, efficiency, and profit come before ethics, morals, and values in a social interplay. We have forgotten what it is like to truly live and enjoy life, without stress and distractions. We don't have time to appreciate the little things in our daily lives, and we are so intent on making money that we forget our own health.

Our daily lives today look totally different from what they were a hundred years ago, and in spite of Internet and globalization we are more isolated from each other now than before. We hand over our children to someone else to be with them during the day while we go to work. When we pick them up in the afternoon it is "the hour of hell" when the children are tired and cranky before they get supper. Afterwards many of us collapse passively by the computer or TV to be fed loads of information, tomorrow's topic of conversation, upsetting us unnecessarily. TVs, computers, and telephones also upset our diurnal rhythm; lack of sleep and being tired is a danger to society. The blue light of the monitors fool our bodies and deprive us of the restorative sleep we need in order to live a life of high quality.

We must become aware of our lifestyle, break destructive patterns, and respect Mother Earth as we once did.

The money goes round and round

Money is the driving engine, constantly circulating. We see what happens in our modern financial world when circulation stops. Some have loads of money and others have none. If the money that is held by the few should start flowing again, we would have a more just world. But money is not everything. It is our time here on Earth that is the most important. A time that is limited and a time many of us spend doing things we'd rather not, just so that we can buy stuff we may not truly need. That is time we can never regain.

How many of us think: if I only had money, I could realize my dreams. Or: when I retire I will have time and money to enjoy life.

Our children grow up without us being quite present, as we keep worrying about money. But how many things do we, and our families, really need? Carpe diem and let's try to spend our time doing things close to our hearts, as often as possible.

Counting the cost

We need a new way of thinking when it comes to the expense, time, and what we pay for. It is said that Time is Money, and it is true in many cases. But if we spend eight to ten hours a day at work and are at home with the family only two hours in the evenings, we may be spending more on things we don't necessarily need. If we cut back on work and spend four hours with the family, our children will be a lot happier and at the same time we may consume less and spare the environment. How do you wish to spend your time?

When we are about to buy something, let's stop and ask ourselves how it got here, how it was made, and how the people who produced it are doing. The closer our relation to a product is, the better we take care of it, and the more grateful we are to have it. It will not be a throw-away. Always look for Fair Trade and ecological labeling.

Save money wisely

When saving money we should check where and how our money is invested. There are ethical funds, supporting sustainability and fair trade that we can choose, rather than investing in alcohol, tobacco, gaming, pornography, weapons, drugs, and the Third World.

There are also Eco-banks, where our savings are managed more transparently and responsibly by people with ecological, social, and cultural values. All loans and credits are published in their brochure and website.

> *"Man. Because he sacrifices his health in order to make money. Then he sacrifices money to recuperate his health. And then he is so anxious about the future that he does not enjoy the present; the result being that he does not live in the present or the future; he lives as if he is never going to die, and then he dies having never really lived."*
>
> *– The Dalai Lama, when asked what surprised him the most about humanity*

Action Now

There is both hope and potential to save and correct what we humans have done to our Mother Earth, but we must hurry. We all need to take small steps in the same direction.

We need to find sustainable solutions in all areas: economy, development, technology, consumption, globalization, travel, research, and education ... and the solutions we work out should preferably endure for seven generations.

WE NEED:

- a new vision of Man as part of Nature, where everyone respects nature and its need for recovery.
- to realize that sustainable agriculture is a cornerstone in all production.
- to minimize emissions from our soils.
- to compost leftover food.
- a sustainable human waste management.
- to drastically reduce consumption.
- new sustainable technology.
- to decrease emissions of carbon dioxides and pollutants.
- to increase local food production and minimize its transportation.
- to see our part in the whole, the eternal cycle; to share with those who have less.

TIP!
globalreporting.org lists companies that dare report their own working conditions, such as child labor for instance.

Children—the new generation

As adults and as parents we have a huge task in raising our children. We must guide them in the right direction and set good examples. Children do as we do, not as we say. If we recycle, the child will learn to do so, too. If we don't buy unnecessary things, they won't either. If we shop at flea markets and secondhand stores, the children will see the advantages and learn to appreciate them too.

It starts in the womb

As women we have to be especially alert to poisons in the environment and in the food we eat. Our bodies store toxins which then are passed on to the child via the umbilical cord. Research has shown that a new born baby may have about 300 chemical toxins in its body, from mercury to amalgam, from hormone-damaging substances to hair coloring agents, and traces of medications.

A varied diet of organically grown fruit and vegetables is best during pregnancy, and so is the need for rest. The arrival of a new child demands mental and physical preparation.

Everything we eat also becomes the baby's food. Same thing with breast feeding. If we smoke, the tar and other toxins in the cigarette pass directly on to the child. Its organs are so small and have to work so hard. Avoid giving the child sugar and gluten, and feed it homemade food as much as possible the first few years—then we know exactly what the child gets.

Clean and toxin-free foods help the baby to develop and grow strong.

Youths

Our children and youths are the ones who will inherit the earth. That's why it is important that we, as parents, but also the schools, take responsibility and start talking about what is happening to our bodies when we live the way we do.

Addiction to gambling among youths has increased and many young people stay up all night drinking energy drinks. This lifestyle can even become a danger to the parents if the kids are not allowed to play. Hormonal balance in teenage girls is disrupted by junk food, sugar, and coloring agents they ingest via fast food and other quick fix food. At worst they may develop an eating disorder interfering with the proper development of their brains and bodies. Child obesity is on the rise all over the world, as is child depression. More and more children and youths are diagnosed with Type 2 diabetes, also known as old age diabetes.

Source: care.diabetesjournals.org

DOWNSHIFTING

Downshifting means exchanging outward wealth with inner wealth. What are money and possessions worth if they rob us of time for what really means something? What is meaningful to you if you cannot slow down and enjoy it?

Slow down!

As a counteraction to the stressful existence many of us experience, several slow-movements have arisen. Among the first was Slow-food, founded in 1989 in Italy to counter the spread of fast food chains and the ever increasing tempo permeating society.

Today Slow-food has branched out across the world to many other areas of our daily lives: slow gardening, slow dancing, slow shopping, etc. But you do not have to join a movement to slow down. Take a walk instead of driving, read a book instead of turning on the TV, eat a home-cooked meal instead of takeout, spend time doing what you enjoy in your free time, learn yoga or meditation, laugh with near and dear, hang out together, talk about life's great mysteries over a cup of tea. Or why not shift down and downsize? If you choose to do everything on a smaller scale; work less, have a smaller house, or shop less, then you will have more time and opportunity to choose how you wish to spend your time.

Live Simpler!

It has now been proven. Too much stuff makes us sick, say the authors of the book Life at Home in the Twenty-First Century, published by University of California, UCLA (2012). This book is the result of a five-year research project, following thirty-two middle-class families in Southern California to see how they cope with our consumer society.

It turns out that after only a few years the families who had recently moved in had filled their closets, drawers, and garage with so much stuff that the car had to be parked in the street, and that it was nearly impossible to get into the kid's room to clean up. In the interviews the families have admitted they feel stressed that they don't have space because of all the stuff. When the researchers measured the parents' levels of the stress hormone cortisol, they found heightened levels in the mothers when they attempted to clear up their cluttered homes.

❗ SEVEN CHALLENGES:

1. Watch the movie *Home* on Youtube.com

2. Look at how you are saving today and where any money is invested.
    Ask questions at the bank and make changes if it does not match your values.

3. Buy only ecologically produced food for one week.

4. Next time you plan to buy something, ask yourself if you really need it.
    Do I have something similar at home? Can I do without this purchase?

5. Read a book or a lovely magazine one night a week instead of watching TV.

6. Make an inventory; can you cut back on work hours? List the effects on your
    consumption vs. your time with the family.

7. Figure three ways that you can contribute on a local or global level.
    For example: volunteer with homeless people, or sending money to children's
    aid organizations.

CHAPTER 2

THE HOME

MAKING SLOW AND SIMPLE CHANGES

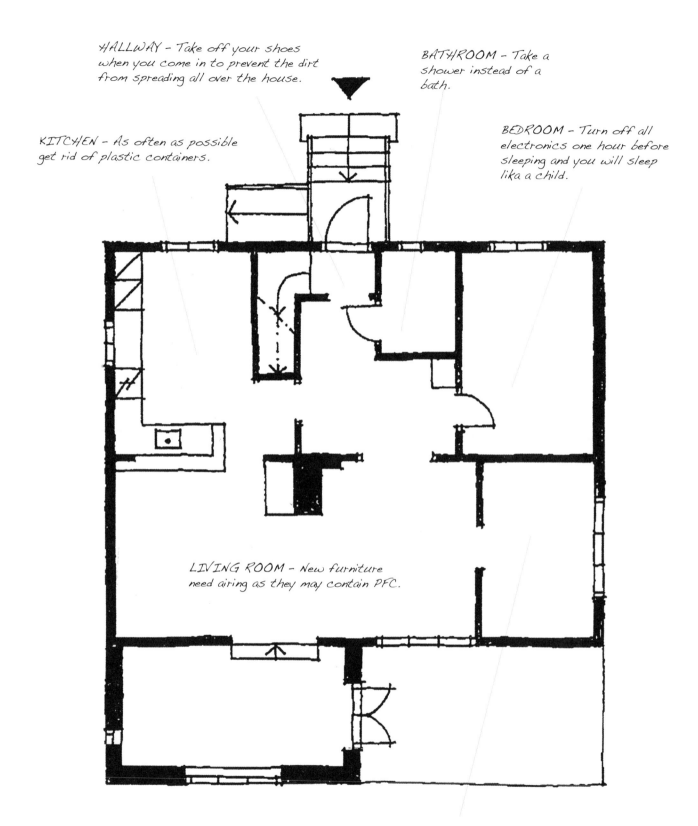

HALLWAY - Take off your shoes when you come in to prevent the dirt from spreading all over the house.

BATHROOM - Take a shower instead of a bath.

KITCHEN - As often as possible get rid of plastic containers.

BEDROOM - Turn off all electronics one hour before sleeping and you will sleep lika a child.

LIVING ROOM - New furniture need airing as they may contain PFC.

CHILDREN'S ROOM - wash toys and plastic objects you already have at home.

The Home

Home—our sanctuary

Our home is a holy place, where we unwind, reenergize, and have a safe, peaceful base. We lock our home to protect it. We don't let just anyone come in. The things in our home are what we have chosen, a reflection of our lives.

If we have a family, the home is a combination of several people getting along in a larger or smaller space. With a family it is even more important to create a space for oneself: a small altar. Altars are common features in all religions and traditions; an altar is a place to worship the greater something you believe in, but also a place for finding courage, trust, and strength.

To live *wabi sabi*

It is said that if we have nice, harmonious surroundings, our souls will also feel good. That does not necessarily mean that we must have new furniture and things. It is easy to amass too many things so that closets, shelves, and drawers overflow.

De-cluttering is a way of freeing up space for the soul. Making room for careful consideration and reflection nurtures our creativity, imagination, and dreams, so we may grow and be able to enjoy life here and now. There is an old Eastern philosophy called *wabi sabi—a* way to live and view the world around us.

Wabi sabi has many aspects and one of them is how we live and see the space around us. It has particular aesthetics to make our home and the place we live more harmonious. What distinguishes *wabi sabi* is that furniture and decor are irregular, have a certain roughness, and are hand-crafted, with soft shapes, of authentic natural materials, simple, and a bit worn. The home is made up of natural objects and furniture is allowed to age gracefully. Nature, and its timeless beauty, is at the root of *wabi sabi*.

In Nature nothing is wasted and Nature only uses the energy it needs. *Wabi sabi* prefers diversity and personality over mass-produced products.

Decorating the home according to *wabi sabi* entails a simple, unassuming style free from trends. It is a decor with few unnecessary items and the items there all have a purpose. We take care of our belongings and mend them when needed. The interiors are of natural materials and the older the better, the more history it has that is meaningful and speaks to us. It is the humble beauty in objects that are important in *wabi sabi*, regardless of defects and shortcomings. Perhaps this philosophy can help us see our home with new eyes: the flaws in the kitchen table, the ring marks on the coffee table, the chips in our favorite mugs, and the water stain on the wooden floor in the hall. *Wabi sabi* emphasizes nostalgia, perhaps even a bitter-sweetness, and the things we keep speak to us of people and memories we cherish. Things we inherited or have kept for a long time hold fascinating stories we are reminded of every time we look at them. Isn't that something worth keeping?

MAKE A PERSONAL ALTAR

- Select a spot where your things will be left alone: a table, a chest, or even a stool.
- Display a photograph of a meaningful moment in your life.
- Put fresh flowers in a vase.
- Light incense or an aromatherapy lamp.
- Place symbols or statues marking your intention in life.
- Light candles.
- Collect pebbles, twigs, and shells you found in Nature.

Visit the altar every day, for whatever little moment you can spare, stop and send a thought of gratefulness that everything is just as it should be—trust in that. You are sacred!

The personal connection is important in *wabi sabi*. Those crocheted pot-holders someone gifted or grandma's old lace curtains—don't they bring back memories in spite of yellowing and rips? *Wabi sabi* means choosing what is worth keeping and what is not, and not buying something for the sake of buying, but to do so because your gut tells you to. Do I need this? Do I like it? Will I use it?

TO FURNISH ACCORDING TO *WABI SABI*

- Make space for the soul, a room for contemplation.
- Be personal, let the favorite vase from grandma stay; it brings back memories.
- Furniture made from natural materials can be recycled.
- No obvious style is visible, yet the furniture and the room fit together in a harmonious and calm atmosphere.
- The furniture is second hand, inherited, used, or flea market finds.
- Choose natural sources of light as far as possible. Light candles to spread warmth and a soft glow.
- Color scheme taken from nature: brown, green, and gray, perhaps with accents in the glorious colors of autumn.
- Follow the seasons and pick the gifts of Nature: flowers, fruits and vegetables, fall anemones, newly chopped firewood, a branch with just opening apple blossoms, or graceful grasses in an empty little bottle.
- Have a mixture of old and new things that are carefully choosen.

Feng Shui

When we get rid of stuff we also let go of what has been and what we have perhaps kept without wanting to. Old, ingrained patterns just hanging on, which we really don't like very much about ourselves. At the same time we get rid of the old we also create space for something new, not just physically, but mentally, too.

Feng Shui is an old, originally Chinese pseudo-science dealing with nature's effect on people, animals, and plants. *Feng Shui* is based in balance and in harmonizing the energy currents in our surroundings. Author Karen Kingston has been practicing *Feng Shui* since the seventies and gives lectures and seminars all over the world.

According to her there are six cornerstones to apply to our daily life to create order out of chaos and make the energy flow through our home in a balanced way.

"If you possess more than 50 things it is the things that possess you."
– Mahatma Gandhi

- Surround yourself with objects you like.
- Everything in its place. Give every thing its own place to live, making it easier to find and not have to waste energy searching for them, while making house cleaning much easier.
- We still live in a society with mail and paper pouring into our homes. Invest in a big waste paper basket and sort the mail, immediately tossing what you don't need. Put whatever is left in nice folders.
- Get rid of unnecessary things and make room. This is when it really matters to be disciplined and cut any emotional ties to objects. Don't save things you believe you may want in the future; it won't happen, trust me. If you have five boxes of the kids' old drawings, baby clothes, shoes, school books, and the like, sort and toss out and I promise that five boxes will soon be three or even two.
- Complete all unfinished projects that otherwise keep nagging you. If you had in mind to fix a broken chair leg, do it. The pictures you meant to hang up, but are still piled up on the floor, hang them and the time you spend thinking about fixing the chair or hanging the pictures, you can now spend on fulfilling your dreams.
- Sort clothes. The clothes you are keeping are those you would bring if you had limited space and were moving overseas, clothes you feel good in.

Stuff costs time

Remember bringing home that new TV? Great picture and great sound, but how long did it take to master the new remote? Or remember when your new shirt turned out to need dry cleaning? Stuff takes time; time you could use planning and developing your dreams. How do you want to spend your time?

Before buying ask:

Do I need this?
How many similar gadgets do I have already?
For how long will I use it?
How has this thing affected the environment?
How will I get rid of it?

Appreciate the simple things in life.

EMF radiation in the home

We are exposed to an unspecified amount of electromagnetic radiation from cell phones, TV sets, computers, and electric cables. This radiation is so recent that we have not yet been able to see the side-effects of all the radiation surrounding us. But it seems quite clear that it affects the body's biochemical processes, which in turn affect nerve signals and other vital functions of the body. Electromagnetic hypersensitivity (EHS) must be taken seriously. We need to take a break from this exposure to realize its harmful effects.

Tech break

Take a break from the computer, telephone, TV, and computer games—try it for a few days or a week and you will notice how much time these gadgets gobble up. Time—which you could use to enhance your uniqueness instead. Make room for something new in your life!

You don't have to pick up the phone, check Facebook, write a text message, surf the web, or listen to music as soon as you have a minute to spare. Dare to take a tech break!

Renovate

The basic rule of renovation is to use eco-labeled paint and lacquers. New, modern paints usually do not contain heavy metals, but the old paint you scrape off may do so. Ventilate well during and after work! Allow the renovated and painted room to air out for a while before using it again, especially important if it is a bedroom that has been repainted. If you are wall-papering, avoid vinyl-treated wallpaper and choose paper. Avoid vinyl flooring, too. Linoleum is a good alternative as it is made from natural materials which wear well and change character naturally with time, looking even better.

Natural paint

Paint made from natural raw materials has been successful for centuries. The principal ingredients are linseed oil, lime from limestone, casein from milk, and natural solvents such as turpentine and/or oils derived from citrus fruit. Chalk and natural pigments make up the remainder. There are now also water-based gloss and satin paints for interior and exterior wood, metal, plaster, and masonry. They may be more expensive, but the benefits are that they contain no fungicides or preservatives. Because they are preservative-free, natural paints do have limited shelf life: about nine months if unopened. Use the same technique for applying natural paints as you would for any other house paint; however, some require longer drying time because they lack chemical drying agents.

Stuff to avoid

Anti-bacterial agents—may be found in detergents, dish rags, cutting boards, stockings, and sportswear to prevent bacteria, mold, and fungus from growing on the products. Use eco-labeled detergents and avoid anti-bacterial agents, which often are very harmful to the environment. Wash clothing and rinse rags before using them.

BISPHENOL – appears to have a number of dangerous effects on health such as brain development, hormones, cancer development of breast and prostate, higher risk for diabetes, cardiovascular diseases, and obesity. Bisphenol A can be found on common receipts, food packaging, and in plastics made from polycarbonates, PCs, as is found in certain toys, lunch boxes, and plastic mugs.

FLAME RETARDANTS – used to extend combustion time of textiles in case of fire. These often contain bromide, similar to PCB, and are absorbed by living organisms. It has been noted that animals have suffered damage to their livers, thyroids, reproduction organs, fetal development, and nervous systems.

FORMALDEHYDE – is a cancer-causing substance used at the end of the production process of conventionally produced cottons and clothing. It is added to keep the fabric smooth during transportation.

PHTHALATES – is a large group of substances, many of which have proved to be hormone disruptors. Phthalates leach out from products containing them, particularly when they are heated. Phthalates may also be found in Glad wrap, disposable gloves, bags, and hoses. Phthalates do not remain in the body, but break down and are secreted, though the secretion may be hormone disruptive and carcinogenic.

NANOPARTICLES – so far we know very little how nanoparticles influence our health and environment as the research is still very recent. Nanoparticles consist of many varied substances with differing properties which make it difficult to ascertain any risks. Some research indicates that inhaling nanoparticles may be harmful and certain nanoparticles are believed to cause lung damage similar to that of asbestos.

POLYCHLORINATED BIPHENYLS (PCB) – PCBs are a group of hazardous contaminants, shown to cause a number of serious cancer and non-cancer health effects in animals and humans, including effects on the immune system, reproductive system, nervous system, endocrine system, and other health effects.

PERFLUORINATED COMPOUNDS (PFCS) – used in "non-stick" cookware such as Teflon, food packaging, and all-weather textiles. PFCs can be transferred via the placenta as well as via breast milk. Studies of PFC exposed animals have shown increased cancer growth in certain organs.

Choose the right material

It is not that easy to live totally toxin-free, but there are alternatives to the biggest eco-villains. Choosing ecological products, that are also Fair Trade-labeled, is a big step toward a greener life. It is not about an end to shopping, but about choosing products and materials carefully and lovingly.

Once you start you will notice how nice it feels to come home with less junk, and with peace of mind knowing what you have chosen to buy is produced in a fair way. Another plus is that products of natural materials and Fair Trade marked, are usually better in quality and are of timeless design, making them fit in better and become more beautiful with time and wear.

BIOPLASTICS – are plastics produced from polylactic acid (PLA) in renewable and biodegradable material from plants like corn, bamboo, sugar cane and rice husks.

MELAMINE – is a kind of hard plastic found in plates, cutlery, and kitchen utensils. The components are toxic, but since they are packed so tightly they do not break down as easily or cause as much damage as, for instance, soft plastics.

FOOD CANS – are lined with bisphenol A. This thin layer is also found in beer and soda cans. Cans that are not lined may leach heavy metals as they are often made with cheap alternatives. Never save food in an opened can, pour the contents into a glass jar if you need to save them.

NATURAL RUBBER – is produced from the sap of rubber trees. To stabilize rubber various components are added in the process which may be hazardous to the workers. There is, however, production that is not harmful and that is controlled.

NATURAL MATERIALS – such as cotton, linen, and silk are in most cases a better choice than a product of synthetic material. If it is also produced ecologically, so much the better! Not only do natural materials feel nicer against the skin, they also decompose easier than synthetic materials.

PAPER – may be treated with bisphenol A to make it water-repellant and grease-resistant as in thermal paper sales receipts. Recycled paper is the better choice.

PLASTICS – contain varying amounts of toxins. Plastic products often have a recycling symbol, a triangle with a number. Take a look at it and, as far as possible, try to avoid the ones with numbers 3 (PVC – polyvinylchloride), 6 (PS-polystyrene), and 7 (PC-polycarbonate) as these components have proven harmful to living organisms.

WOOD – is a perfect natural material as long as it is not painted or lacquered. Before you buy treated wood, try to find out what kind of paint was used. You can treat your wood furniture yourself with linseed oil wax, which is natural.

TEXTILES – should be chosen with care. To make one cotton T-shirt, well over 1 000 gallons of water and a lot of chemicals are used. Even dyed cloth contains lots of chemicals that not only remain, but also are leached out in nature during the process. Avoid clothing that is heavily dyed. Today there is ecologically-produced cotton, but you can't always trust one resource. Bamboo, hemp, and linen are alternative materials. These are fast-growing crops with minimal effects in the soil. Eco-alternatives are still better as there are always producers who still use biocides.

RECYCLING – is of course the very best for the environment as the environmental impact of the production process is already done. To conserve the environment for future generations we must cut back on our consumption. If we still want new furniture, clothes, and stuff, buying secondhand is an alternative. The benefits are a more personal style and a greener footprint. Take a look at www.ebay.com and www.amazon.com to swap, buy, or sell.

TIP!
Say no to things you don't want. By adopting JOMO, joy of missing out, you will have more time and a less stressful life.

TIP!
Embrace Slow Shopping. In other words, think before you buy. That way you may avoid impulse buying you would later regret.

TIP!
Say no to receipts. 40 percent of all receipts you usually get contain the chemicals bisphenol A (BPA). If you must have a receipt, ask for one via email that you can print out on a safe printer and paper.

Home furnishings

We are surrounded by toxic substances of which we may not be aware. Our furniture, our kids' toys, clothes, and electronics all contain chemicals that give off fumes or leach, especially when they are brand new. But there are ways of avoiding this.

- Follow your nose: if it smells of chemicals—don't buy it!
- Throw out all old plastic toys, even cuddlies with plastic details.
- Wash toys and plastic objects you already have at home.
- When you unwrap new furniture, make sure to air out thoroughly.
- Avoid furniture that may be treated with PFCs and flame retardants. Imitation leathers sometimes contain phthalates.
- Keep in mind that even old upholstered furniture may contain flame retardants.
- Home electronics like TVs, computers, and cell phones contain flame retardants and phthalates. These compounds may be released when in use and getting warm, so make sure to turn them off when you don't need them.
- Buy eco-labeled products when possible.
- Clean and air out regularly to minimize the spread of chemicals in the air.

Have a healthy house

- A simple way to create cleaner air indoors is to place potted green plants in every room. They even help to absorb chemical emissions. The peace lily is a particularly effective plant. Dried sage is also good in cleaning the air.
- Invest in an aroma lamp and essential oils. Read more about essential oils on *page 81*.
- Make your own room spray with distilled water and your favorite essential oil. Use aroma therapy. Take 4 fl oz of water and 10 drops essential oil.

TIP!
It is important to vacuum and dust every week to keep chemicals in furniture and belongings down to a minimum!

Clean house without chemicals

Instead of different miracle cleansers with loads of chemicals to help you clean, take a look in your pantry. There are a whole bunch of things you can use for cleaning your home.

These natural cleaners have several advantages; the ingredients are easy to obtain, inexpensive and have no damaging effect on the environment, they contain no additives, so are unlikely to cause allergic reactions, they are not tested on animals, and they come in recyclable packaging.

Useful ingredients for homemade cleaners:

SOAP NUTS – a 100 percent natural detergent without chemical additives. Soap nuts are the fruits of large trees you find, among other places, in India and Nepal. The trees contribute to the oxygenation of the soil.

The fruits contain saponins, Nature's own detergent. When the fruit skin is in contact with water it excretes a mild, cleansing and non-allergenic foam which is gentle on both skin and textiles, suitable for baby's tender skin.

Soap nuts are actually a fruit and can be used by those allergic to nuts. Leftovers can be composted. Soap nuts may be used for washing clothes, cars, hair, and can give a shine to gold and silver jewelery. Add 1 tbsp bicarbonate to white laundry to bleach it a bit. 2lbs of soap nuts is enough for 2–3 laundry loads a week.

CUT BACK ON THESE CHEMICALS

CHLORINE – most dishwasher detergents contain chlorine, a disinfectant, in its dry form. This releases toxic fumes into the kitchen, which can cause headaches, burning eyes, and breathing difficulties.

PHOSPHATES – may be found in wool washing agents, multi-purpose cleaners, dishwasher powders, and scouring cleaners. Phosphates are responsible for excessive growth of algae in the water systems.

BLEACHES – most household bleaches are based on sodium hypochlorite, which has a known effect on hormone levels. Bleached toilet paper, kitchen towels, and facial tissues contain residues of toxic dioxins and brighteners.

TABLE SALT – Place your silver jewelery on a sheet of aluminium foil and add plenty of ordinary salt. Cover with hot water. A voltaic element is formed causing all oxides (the black stuff) to dissolve from the silver, making it nice and shiny again. Cheap and eco-friendly.

WHITE VINEGAR – is a naturally-produced acid that forms when wine is left standing for a few weeks. It dissolves calcium and can be used in cleaning the dishwasher. Put a cup of white vinegar in an otherwise empty dishwasher and run your normal program, to loosen detergent residues and calcium deposits.

CITRUS FRUIT – has a naturally cleansing and bleaching juice, and in combination with salt even more effective. Cut a lemon or grapefruit in half. Use one half like a sponge on the kitchen counter to make the stainless steel shine. Use the other half in the bathtub to scrub away calcium and soap deposits. Boost the scrubbing effect by sprinkling salt on the cut surface.

A few slices of lemon in a bowl of water help clean the microwave oven without using harsh chemicals. Warm the bowl on full effect for 3 minutes and the citrus fumes will clean the oven. Wipe dry with paper.

Lemon also removes stains and freshens cutting boards.

PINE SOAP – a green liquid pure soap, good for much more than just washing the floor. For example, smear the inside of the oven with green soap, heat to 212F (100C). When cooled off, rinse with sponge and water. Boil water with a bit of green soap to help clean scorched saucepans.

BAKING SODA – is a versatile cleanser that can also be used to clean the toilet bowl from dirt and calcium, as well as getting rid of brown stains in coffee mugs.

BICARBONATE – can handle clogged drains. Pour a ¼ of a cup of bicarbonate and a ¼ of a cup of white wine or vinegar into the drain and let sit for a while before you flush with hot water. You can use bicarbonate to clean the washing machine by running it without laundry with ¼ cup of bicarbonate instead of laundry detergent.

Use bicarbonate to keep ants out, to get rid of nasty smells, stains, and much more.

LAVENDER – keeps moths away. Put dried lavender in linen cupboard, closets, and drawers.

TIP!
Always wash new clothes at least three times before wearing them, in order to get rid of any chemicals.

Better cleaning – clean suggestions!

Window cleaner 1

1 part water
1 part white vinegar
A few drops liquid soap

Mix all in a jar with a lid.

Window cleaner 2

Take a bucket of warm water and add a little eco-dishwashing liquid. Wash the windows with a rag. Squeegee off excess water and dry with newspaper for a shiny finish.

All-purpose cleaner

3 tbsp white vinegar
20 drops tea tree oil
20 drops essential orange oil
2 cups warm water

Mix everything in a spray bottle and spray where needed and dry with lint-free cloth. This works best in the kitchen on faucets, sink, stove, in the refrigerator etc. Smells very fresh, works well on calcium and lime deposits and various stains, is anti-bacterial and eco-friendly to boot, and may safely be used on food preparation surfaces.

Polish

4 tbsp water
4 tbsp baking soda

Apply with a rag and chrome, aluminium surfaces, pots and pans, and fridge interiors become sparkling clean.

TIP!
Save old toothbrushes—they are perfect for cleaning in tight areas.

Bathroom spray

Peel a citrus fruit (lime, lemon, orange, or grapefruit—or make a mixture) and place the peel in a bowl. Add white wine vinegar. Let stand and steep. Strain off the peel and pour the mixture in to an empty spray bottle to use on bathroom porcelain.

Toilet bowl cleaner

Pour 1–3 capfuls of white vinegar into the bowl. Let it sit a while, then brush with toilet bowl brush and flush. Dirt and calcium deposits are gone! So are the bacteria. Disinfect with tea tree oil in the water for about 30 minutes. Flush.

Bathtub

Have a problem with ingrained dirt in the tub? Cut a grapefruit in half, put salt on the cut, and scrub the tub. The grapefruit contains an acid that cuts through the dirt, and the combination of salt and acid makes the fruit an effective scrubber.

Or put the peel of an orange, lemon, or lime in a jar and add white wine vinegar. Let steep, strain, and use in a spray bottle as power cleanser on porcelain, removing even stubborn stains.

Bathroom tiles

Use bicarbonate and water to scrub the tiles. Tiles get nice and clean if you first scrub with scrubbing sponge and water with a bit of dishwashing liquid. Rinse with clean water spiked with a few tablespoons of cornstarch. Polish with a lint-free cloth. The cornstarch gets rid of the last remnants of grease.

Steam iron

Clean the holes underneath with a Q-tip dipped in white vinegar.

Stove

Mix baking soda with white vinegar (it will fizzle), and pour the mixture around the burners on the top of the stove. Let soak before you wash clean with sponge and water.

Exhaust fan and vents

Regular cleaning of the kitchen fan is important, mainly to avoid bacteria falling into the food. Clean the filters at least once a month, preferably every two weeks. Wash in warm water with a mild detergent or in the dishwasher.

Vents can be cleaned easily with a cloth dipped in warm water and soap. Wrap the cloth around a knife to get at the tight spots, and the dirt will come off easily.

Smelly fridge

Cure a smelly fridge by simply pouring some carbonated water in a mug and place inside. The soda water absorbs the smell.

Mattresses

In spite of spending a third of our lives sleeping, how often do we think of cleaning the mattress we sleep on? A mattress absorbs over a cup of perspiration every night, so before you vacuum the mattress, dust it with bicarbonate.

The bicarbonate contains crystals that are drier than anything else in its surroundings, causing the crystals to absorb the moisture from the mattress. Wait twenty minutes and then vacuum. Flip the mattress over and do the other side the same way—hey, presto, home dry-cleaning!

Wooden furniture

Eco-friendly furniture polish:

¼ cup fresh squeezed lemon juice
½ cup olive oil (organic oil if you desire a totally eco-polish)

Pour the ingredients into a jar, close the lid, and shake vigorously. Done! Dry and polish with lint-free cloth.

Smelly dishwasher

Spread coffee beans in the machine and let stand closed for a day. Remove the beans before using again.

Floor cleaning

Invest in a floor mop with a microfibre cloth and give the vacuum cleaner a rest. Scrub the floors by hand with natural soap and water. If the floor has tough stains, get down on your knees and scrape to the sound of good music.

TIP!

Invest in a polishing cloth with microfibres. It can be washed hundreds of times!

CONSERVE WATER

- Wash up in the sink.
- Avoid washing under running water.
- Run the dishwasher only when full and on lowest heat setting.
- Halve the amount of dishwasher detergent—especially tablets, it will still get clean.
- Shower instead of taking a bath.
- Turn off the water while lathering.

Reduce waste!

- Bring a cloth bag, or reuse plastic bags when shopping.
- Buy fruit and vegetables in bulk if possible.
- If you are out and about, bring simple cutlery instead of using plastic. You can get cutlery made of wood in travel kits.
- Compost.
- Sort garbage and recycle as much as possible. Be active in the community and push for recycling in your area.
- Shop less and often to avoid throwing out food. The food waste is a huge eco-villain.
- Buy herbs and other veggie plants in pots that can be recycled.
- Avoid buying canned food.
- Return glass and plastic bottles and get your deposit back.
- Instead of tossing clothes, children's stuff, books etc, donate to a charity, rent a table at a flea market, have a yard sale, join a swap meet, or sell on the Internet.

What to recycle:

COMPOST – If you live in a house you can have your own compost. The soil it generates you can then use in your own garden. Read more on *page 99*.

PAPER – Sort newspapers and cardboard.

PLASTICS.

GLASS – Separate clear and coloured glass.

BATTERIES.

LIGHT BULBS.

HALOGEN LIGHTS.

LARGE ITEMS – chairs, shelves, carpets.

REUSE JUNK!

- Refurbish and give away! Decorate old ladles, frames, or paint old tables—like new!
  Read more about green gifts on *page 117*.
- Paint fruit crates and turn them into shelves.
  Arrange them into a practical shelf for shoes by the front door.
- Use PET bottles as planters for seedlings.

Kitchen

Plastics are a scourge of our health and environment. Plastics contain a number of substances called obesogens—dietary, pharmaceutical, and industrial compounds that may alter metabolic processes and make some people gain weight. But there are ways to avoid ingesting these compounds:

- Never allow warm food to be in contact with plastic as the heat may cause phthalates to be released.
- Get rid of non-stick and Teflon cookware and avoid plastic water kettles.
- Don't buy micro-popcorn in bags lined with plastic.
- Exchange plastic thermoses for metal ones.
- When possible, get rid of plastic food containers.
- Exchange plastic lunch boxes for one of glass or metal.
- Don't put plastic-wrapped food in the fridge. Use an inverted plate or bowl instead.
- Avoid food in cans as they often contain hormone-disruptive bisphenol A.

TIP!
On www.ecolunchboxes.com you will find eco-friendly lunch and storage containers.

Store food safely

- Make sure fridge and freezer keep the proper temperature; the fridge should be 37 degrees and the freezer about 3 degrees (F). Put chilled products in the fridge as soon as you come home from shopping. Most vegetables and fruit last longer if kept in the fridge.
- Freeze food you want to keep for a longer period. Look, smell, and taste before you throw out food past the Best Before date. Use leftovers; make a pick'n'eat meal, create a new dish, or freeze.
- Fruit and veggies are being thrown out the most, usually because we buy more than we can eat, and because we haven't stored it properly. Refrigerate what you do not intend to eat the same day!
- Make a fruit salad or smoothie of overripe fruit. Wilted vegetables can be added to a stew or omelet. Put lettuce, carrots, and other limp roots in a bowl of water for a few hours in the fridge and they will get crisp and crunchy again.

- Fruit and berries can be frozen, but first cut them into smaller pieces. Vegetables can be frozen if you parboil them first, i.e. boil water, put the veggies in to cook for a moment and then chill them quickly under running cold water. Berries, fruit, and veggies will keep for a year or more in the freezer. Bacteria do not grow in the freezer, so old food is not dangerous, but it may dry out and lose taste and texture.
- Oils can be stored at room temperature, but preferably in a dark place to avoid sunlight which makes it go rancid. Keeping oil cool will make it last even longer. Some oils, like olive oil, turn solid if kept in the fridge, but regain their liquid form in room temperature.

Bathroom

The bathroom is the place where we get clean and refreshed, where we begin and end the day. Give your bathroom a facelift of its own and you will feel revived and happier, too. Old creams, half empty toothpaste tubes, and dirt often collect under the sink, so now it is time to get rid of all you don't need.

Read the suggestions for house cleaning to get an even greener bathroom, make your own lotions, and purchase natural cotton towels and an aroma lamp.

CONSERVE WATER
1. Turn off the water while you brush your teeth.
2. Install a low flush toilet and you will save 1 gallon of water each flush. You can even install this in your old toilet.
3. Take a shower instead of a bath.

Living room

We often have lots of electronics in our living rooms. These contain flame retardants which are emitted when the appliances are left on. Turn off and unplug them when you are not watching TV or listening to music. That goes for the computer, too.

Empty battery chargers should not be left plugged in because of harmful emissions and they may self-ignite. Upholstered new furniture need airing as they may contain PFCs. Even imitation leather contains phthalates. Buy secondhand—most of the chemicals have already been aired out.

Man-made fibers may now dominate the textile market, but natural fabrics—especially those derived from organic sources and colored with natural dyes—are better for our health and sense of well-being, and are far gentler on the environment. Although more expensive than synthetic fibers, good quality natural fabrics are perhaps a better investment in the long run as we are more inclined to take care of them and repair them before throwing them out. To maintain soft furnishings in pristine condition, always read the care label instructions before cleaning.

Bedroom

In the bedroom we relax, sleep, and have sex.
The bedroom should be considered a holy place for wonderful restorative sleep and we really shouldn't bring work, watch TV, web surf, or have telephones in the bedroom.

Try to remove electric gadgets all together and invest instead in an old style alarm clock. Furnish the room with as few pieces as possible and keep the colors light. The bedroom is a place for sleep, not a place to spend most of your waking time. It is a way to signal the body that it is sleep that matters here. Read more about sleep in the Raw food section.

Use soft lighting, preferably an aroma lamp with soothing essential oils, a beautiful little book to write down the day's happenings, and some light reading. The bedroom is also the place for lust and passion. To keep that flowing in an eco-friendly way, read *page 59.*

Good bedding for good sleep!

For a healthy sleep choose a cotton mattress or an organic cotton, linen, or wool futon. Wool is particularly suitable for bedding, because it both insulates and absorbs humidity well—the body produces considerable amounts of moisture during sleep. To protect the mattress from perspiration and soiling, cover it with a natural mattress pad.

Synthetic fibers do not "breathe" and so are often uncomfortably hot to sleep in. Bedclothes made from natural materials, linen, cotton, hemp, and bamboo help regulate your body temperature while you sleep so that you do not become too hot. Natural fabrics also feel soft to touch. Buy organic unbleached cotton, cotton flannel, muslin, or linen sheets and pillowcases.

TIP!

Wash bed linen 3 times at 104 degrees before making the bed to get rid of any chemicals that may be allergenic.

Sleep more!

To sleep, rest, and recuperate is not laziness. In today's society it is, strangely enough, shameful to sleep a lot. You are lazy, don't take responsibility, and don't do anything with your life. But sleep is one of the cornerstones we need to live. While we sleep our cells recover and renew energy. Lack of good sleep does not improve life. The best time for sleep is between 9 pm and 5 am. The hours before midnight provide the best healing, when liver and kidneys are working their hardest, and sorting the events of the day in the form of dreams.

To be able to cope during the day we trick the body into alertness with the help of nicotine, caffeine, and simple carbohydrates, but that works only for a short time. The body can't go on like that. It can become a vicious circle, drinking coffee at night, a sleeping pill to be able to sleep, and then having to drink even more coffee the next morning, just to get going. A power nap is one way of re-energizing, but the best is still to sleep 8–10 hours a night.

TIP!

Turn off all electronics one hour before sleeping to clear your energy field and sleep much better.

Clean sex

Sex is part of life and to prevent getting pregnant there have been, for centuries, different ways to protect oneself. During the last 70 years it has mostly been the woman taking the Pill or by using a spiral. But there are natural, and free, alternatives to prevent an unwanted pregnancy without women having to pop hormone pills, which may have side effects for both body and environment.

THE BILLINGS METHOD

is based on the woman's ability to know when her fertile periods begin and end. She can thus avoid or enable a pregnancy. The method was developed by Evelyn and John Billings, both doctors, in Australia in the 1960s. By observing her discharges and keeping notes, the woman becomes aware of her menstrual cycle's various secretions and is able to figure out when ovulation and the fertile period are happening. According to the World Health Organization (WHO), 90 percent of all women are able to tabulate their own fertility after one month of observation. The method is used diligently by Catholics and other societies that do not allow contraceptives, but is suitable for all who want natural sex.

THE RHYTHM METHOD

is another quite natural method for avoiding penetration during the fertile days. Instead of keeping notes of discharges as in the Billings method, the rhythm method is based on previous menstrual cycles. You can also use a thermometer to check your temperature as it usually rises half a degree directly after ovulation. The rhythm method is more unreliable than the Billings method.

COITUS INTERRUPTUS

is the classic method to avoid full penetration, but is relatively unreliable as you must stop at the right moment.

DIAPHRAGM

is a cap of silicon placed in the vagina covering the cervical entrance. Preferably used together with spermicide.

FERTILITY MONITOR

is a contraceptive device calculating safe days, usually based on body temperature or hormone levels. There are also monitors measuring the hormone level in the urine, and those that measure the hormone level via changes in temperature. There are variations depending on which monitor is used. The advantage of a monitor is that it helps you keep track of ovulation in a simple and easy way without affecting the body physically. The disadvantage may be that its calculations and estimates are based on the "average woman's" menstrual cycle which may not be applicable for everyone. It may lead to a false sense of security. The fertility monitor, like the Billings method, is based on preventing penetration when there is a risk of pregnancy.

BREAST-FEEDING

is the world's most common method of contraception. It is believed that since ovulation does not occur during the time you nurse, you can not get pregnant. This method is only certain during the first six months after birth; nursing must be total and problem-free, meaning the baby is breastfed at every meal and menstruation must not have resumed. Note that once menstruation resumes, ovulation occurred two weeks earlier, with an infertile egg causing the first menstruation after giving birth. Theoretically you could become pregnant before menstruation resumes.

Clothes

Most of us have clothing we have only used once. That is not okay. It is better to buy secondhand for a personal style. Taking care of our clothes, altering, or mending is a smart way to make clothes last longer.

GET SMART!

- Why not organize a clothes swapping day, *clothingswap.com* or visit a clothing "library." Use Google to find the nearest one in your area.
- Buy clothing in thrift stores or vintage shops.
- Hang out to air instead of washing.
- Avoid buying clothes that need dry-cleaning.
- Turn clothes inside out when washing to keep colors lasting longer.
- Use soap nuts and essential oils instead of laundry detergents and fabric softeners. The latter is very carcinogenic.
- Wash your clothes with Laundry Balls.
- Wash less often. The cleaner food you eat, the less you perspire.

GOODBYE STAIN!

- To remove stains, try gall soap.
- Lemon is also an effective stain remover.
- To remove grass stains, grease, and make-up use eucalyptus oil.
- Sometimes it is worthwhile using a chemical stain remover to get rid of a small stain, instead of throwing the whole thing out. Think large scale!

TIP!

Avoid buying clothes that need dry-cleaning. Dry-cleaning emits toxins and leaves a residual coating which is why you need to air the clothes that have been dry-cleaned. If you absolutely have to dry-clean something, choose an eco-friendly cleaning company.

! SEVEN CHALLENGES:

1. Turn off all electronics an hour before bedtime for one week and see how much better you will sleep.

2. Check email only once a day.

3. Download the app Find Recycling and find the nearest location.

4. Make your own room spray.

5. Care for your house plants or buy new ones.

6. Sort through your closet, give away or plan a clothes swapping day with stuff you no longer want to keep.

7. Clear out piles of stuff in the attic, basement, and garage.

Make your own dry shampoo, page 86.

Brighten dark circles with chamomile tea, page 87.

Oat mask with honey for more bliss in your face, page 81.

Relaxing bath for your body with cardamon seeds, page 84.

Happy feet with flake salt and sesame oil, page 84.

THE BODY

GOING FROM CHEMICALS TO NATURAL

A mashed avocado is a lovely moisturizer for the face.

Our skin

Did you know that the skin is our largest organ? It is almost 21 square feet and weighs between eight to ten pounds. Its thickness varies on the different body parts.

The skin has many different functions: to protect the underlying tissues, to repel water, to protect, to regulate body temperature, to secrete toxins, and to breathe. In order for the skin to breathe we must make sure it does not get clogged by things that prevent oxygenation and sloughing off waste. If the skin becomes clogged, then the tissues beneath will also become clogged. It has been said that the skin is the body's second kidney and that it relieves the pressure on the kidneys by sweating. It is important that we perspire so that we get rid of substances the body needs to excrete. There are many ways to help the skin to effectively sweat out stuff the body doesn't need. Certain drinks and food can boost perspiration. Touch, massage, and scrubbing also increase blood circulation making cleansing more effective.

The skin is also a part of our immune defence. The outermost layer consists mainly of dead skin cells, sebum, and sweat, and together they form a protective barrier. If what is inside the body can get out through the skin by sweating, then that means that what we put on our skin can also get into the body. It is not only what we put in our mouths, but also what we put on our skin. You could almost say the skin eats what it gets.

How do you wish to feed your skin?

Conventional skin care, which is the most common today and the one with which many of us are familiar, is based on petroleum products, such as kerosene, gasoline, mineral oil, and plastics. Most of them are also chock-full of various types of synthetic preservatives to prolong their shelf life. You could compare conventional skin care with a tomato, sprayed with chemical biocides to keep it looking fresh for as long as possible. But who wants to eat a two week old tomato? Fresh and clean produce is what is best for the body.

Conventional skincare products are made from finite resources which are difficult for the body to break down, as they contain compounds that are harmful to both us and the environment.

On *page 69* is a list of the most common substances to avoid putting on your skin. But more and more skincare products are turning up which make both our bodies and Mother Earth happy. On *page 89* are lots of examples of brands respectful of the total production cycle.

One pointer for choosing skincare products: look for the USDA mark guaranteeing the purity of the product.

When you begin to exchange your usual lotions, shampoos, and deodorants for natural alternatives, it may take a while for the body to detox. During this time skin may become drier and feel rough, hair may feel dirty and greasy quicker, and perspiration under the arms may smell bad now that waste and toxins can actually leave the body, whereas the pores were blocked by aluminum-based deodorants before. Be patient and give your body the time it needs.

If you do not wish to buy ready-made skincare, just use what you have in the pantry. Making your own is better for environment and body, and you will know for certain what you rub into your skin.

What is in the skincare products?

In the US and Canada, also in the EU, it has been decided that cosmetics must have a list of ingredients that is the same for all countries. To that purpose a catalogue of common names of substances was issued, called INCI, International Nomenclature of Cosmetic Ingredients. The INCI lists all plant-based ingredients with their Latin names, which perhaps makes it hard to recognize and understand the natural components. On product labels they are listed in descending order, meaning the greatest amount is at the top of the list.

TIP!

A rule-of-thumb: the shorter the list, the purer the product!

TIP!

Apply sunflower or olive oil on your lips to keep them soft. Organic coconut oil also works well.

Questionable substances

Conventional cosmetics often contain synthetic substances, some of which have turned out to be harmful to humans and environment. Here is the list of the most common ones. Good to know!

ALUMINUM CHLORIDE (INCI NAME: ALUMINUM CHLOROHYDRATE) – an aluminum salt used in most deodorants. It has an anti-perspiring effect as it blocks the pores. Using this every day in the sensitive armpit, which is also shaved, is not quite safe.

BUTYLACETATE/BUTYLETHANOATE – (INCI NAME: SILICON/DIMETHICONE/ DIPHENYL DIMETHICONE/METHICONE) – a solvent, and the most common ingredient found in nail polish. Makes sunscreens waterproof and lipstick "kiss-proof." It is considered harmful to the nervous system.

PHTHALATES (INCI NAME: ALCOHOL DENAT PERFUME) – is ordinary alcohol that has been denatured in order to make it undrinkable. It is found in perfumes and skincare products. Animal tests have shown that several phthalates are toxic to the reproductive system, liver, kidney, and lungs.

MINERAL OIL (INCI NAME: MINERAL OIL, MEDICAL WHITE OIL, OLEUM PETROLEUM, PARAFFIN, PARAFFINUM LIQUIDUM, OLEUM VASELINE, VASELINE, KEROSENE, PETROLEUM, PROPYLENE, AND WHITE MINERAL OIL) – is a by-product of the distillation of petroleum and is found in almost all conventional cosmetics today. Just hearing the name you would think it was something that was good for the body, but mineral oil contains nothing of value for skin, body, nature, or animals.

SODIUM LAURYL SULPHATE (INCI NAME: SODIUM LAURYL SULPHATE /SLS/, SODIUM LAURETH SULPHATE/SLES/) – is a common surfactant making soaps and shampoos bubble and foam. Surfactants are both water- and grease-repellent. SLS does not only dissolve dirty grease, but also the skin's protective oil. This should be used with caution and should not be more than a small percent of the total content in products. It is also found in toothpaste where it may cause tiny holes in the mucous membranes of the mouth, which means that it is next to impossible to avoid absorbing it when brushing our teeth. Should not be high up on the list of ingredients, and should not be used by small children!

PEG (INCI NAME: POLYETHYLENE GLYCOL PEG 50 STEARATE) – is a synthetic emulsifier and moisture-carrier, allowing water and oil to mix. PEG also functions as a moisturizer in liquid soap, stabilizing the foam. PEGs don't break down easily in the environment and have proven negative health effects.

PROPYLENE GLYCOL (INCI NAME: PROPYLENE GLYCOL) – like PEGs, functions as a penetration enhancer and can allow harmful ingredients to be absorbed more readily through the skin. It can also cause allergic reactions. It is an alcohol distilled from propylene oxide which is derived in several stages from petroleum.

SILICONES (INCI NAME: OFTEN END IN –CONE, -CONOL, AND –XANE) – form a film clogging skin and hair.

SYNTHETIC PERFUMES (INCI NAME: FRAGRANCE, PERFUME) – are made from unknown synthetic chemicals. Most synthetic perfumes contain phthalates, believed to cause reproductive problems. Keep in mind that even natural perfumes based on essential oils may also be allergenic.

TRIETHANOLAMINE AND DIETHANOLAMINE (INCI NAME: TEA, DEA AND TRIETHANOLAMINE STEARATE, TRIETHANOLAMINE LAURYL SULPHATE) – produced from petroleum by-products. It has been used for decades as an emulsifier in cosmetics. It is an eye and skin irritant.

TRICLOSAN – is an anti-bacterial agent, toxic to the environment, and has been found in sewage treatment plants.

EUXYL K 100 (INCI NAME: BENZYL ALCOHOL, METHYLCHLOROISOTHIA-ZOLINONE, METHYLISOTHIAZOLINONE) – is a preservative that can cause blisters, boils, itching, rash, and swellings in the skin.

ACTIZIDE AC (INCI NAME: METHYLCHLOROISOTHIAZOLINONE, METHYLISOTHIA-ZOLINONE) – is a preservative. This is usually the reason you are sensitive to a product.

POTASSIUM SORBATE (INCI NAME: POTASSIUM SORBATE) – is a preservative to which many people are sensitive.

PARABENS (INCI NAME: METHYLPARABEN, BUTYLPARABEN, ETHYLPARABEN, PROPYLPARABEN, ISOBUTYLPARABEN) – are effective preservatives in many types of formulas. They are used primarily for their bactericidal and fungicidal properties. They can be found in shampoos, commercial moisturizers, shaving gels, and toothpastes. There is evidence that they interfere with hormone function.

TIP!

Start exchanging the products you use the most and that are applied directly on the skin and are not rinsed off like for example: facial cream, deoderant, and body lotion.

THESE ARE NATURAL COSMETICS:

- The ingredients must be plant-based, wild or organically grown.
- Animal parts may not be used. Animal testing is absolutely forbidden.
- No synthetic aroma- or coloring-agents.
- Preservation must be only by natural or bio-identical substances.
- No ionized radiation to sterilize products.
- Mineral oils and silicones are not permitted.
- The raw materials must be biologically degradable.
- Production and packaging must have minimal effect on the environment.
- Opposition to genetic manipulation.
- When possible, the organic raw produce should be grown on Fair Trade certified farms.
- Transparent and complete declaration of contents.
- Certification by independent testing laboratory.

Source: *turkos.se*

The reasons for using natural cosmetics

Natural cosmetics are based on love and respect for Nature and a holistic view of humans and the environment. Body lotions and other skincare products that are natural only contain renewable raw materials and are made from cold-pressed vegetable oils together with valuable essential oils and herbs.

The ingredients are derived from plants, wild or organically grown, and are biologically degradable. Their production is built on old knowledge of using flowers, herbs, and cold-pressed vegetable oils to make skincare products that actually care for the skin.

From time immemorial we have made use of natural resources to beautify and care for our bodies. Today natural cosmetics are not only trendy, but the only sustainable alternative for a natural beauty.

Many conventional brands claim to be natural although they contain questionable ingredients. It is therefore important to read the list of contents before you buy it. The product should preferably also be certified by an independent organization who can verify that it contains no chemical or synthetic substances.

Why use organic skincare product?

Our skin is, as we said earlier, the largest organ, and it actually absorbs more than 65 percent of the stuff we smear on it. Organic ingredients contain lots of antioxidants, important vitamins, and nutrients. Antioxidants help prevent signs of aging without causing harmful side-effects, which occasionally have been associated with non-organic ingredients.

TIP!

Relax and your skin will glow. Lower expectations, prioritize exercise and sleep, eat regularly, do what you enjoy, and laugh a lot.

Organic labeling

USDA certified organic products are produced without synthetic preservatives, petrochemicals, ionized radiation, or biocides. USDA, United States Department of Agriculture, has set a national standard for organic labeling.

In order to be allowed to use the USDA seal the product must contain 95 percent organically produced ingredients. USDA has four categories for labeling purposes based on the amount of organic content.

1. A product claiming to be 100 percent organic must contain only organically-produced ingredients and processing aids.

2. A product claiming to be organic must contain at least 95 percent organically-grown produce, and must not be produced using synthetic preservatives, petrochemicals, ionizing radiation, or other prohibited methods.

3. 70–95 percent organic, labeled "Made with Organic Ingredients," can contain just about anything in the 5–30 percent of ingredients that are not organic. They can be grown with pesticides, but not the sewage sludge, and cannot be irradiated or contain genetically modified organisms (GMO).

4. Less than 70 percent, labeled "Contains Organic Ingredients" may have all kinds of undesirable things in that 30 percent content. Who knows?!

Why choose USDA certified products?

The only way customers can be somewhat certain that they get certified organic products made without synthetic chemicals, is to buy products carrying the USDA seal.

TIP!

Remember that skincare products are not necessarily natural even if they claim to be. Cast a critical eye on the list of contents.

Deodorants

It is quite normal to perspire under the arms and it is not the sweat itself that smells bad, but the bacteria that forms when perspiration ferments. In the old days it was thought that if you tried to prevent sweating you were begging for illness, as the sweat would then turn inwards. Today certain studies have shown a connection to aluminum in anti-perspirants and breast cancer. Other research does not support that hypothesis.

What we do know is that aluminum chloride and aluminum chlorohydrate get into the pores and clog the sweat glands. The molecules continue on to the blood and it is suspected that they affect the body's aluminum levels. Today we have several alternatives without these chemicals. When you exchange your conventional deodorant for an organic one, be patient until your body gets used to doing without the chemicals. Many deodorants also contain alcohol which can be dehydrating. Choose a deodorant, without aluminum, that contains organic alcohol.

DIY deodorant

3 tbsp organic coconut oil
2 tbsp bicarbonate
2 tbsp cornstarch
1 drop essential oil, for example bergamot

Mix the dry ingredients in a glass jar with a lid. Add the oil, which should be solid. Add the bergamot and mix the paste with a teaspoon. Take a dab and rub between your fingers and apply under your arm. Keep the deodorant cool or the coconut oil will melt.

TIP!
Elderberry tea helps clean out waste. Perspiration increases, stimulating the immune system.

TIP!
Go to a sauna and rid the body of waste and other chemical residues as the sweat glands are going at full speed in the heat.

Green veggies, fresh fruit, nuts, and omega-3 fatty acids also help cleanse the body from inside.

Skin—up close and personal

Essential oils are fragrant, fugitive oils found in various plant parts. Essential oils may be composed of many different chemical compounds. Many can be produced synthetically and are present in cosmetics that are not organic or natural.

Natural scents

All essential oils have their own unique composition, which means that they all have different specific characteristics. Essential oils have several beneficial health effects on body and soul. Fugitive oils form in certain parts of the leaf and flower of various plants, and are collected through distillation or pressing. Pure essential oils should not be applied directly on the skin; they should be blended with creams or other natural oils first. Their effective fragrance may be diffused with the help of an aroma lamp.

Put a few drops of essential oil in a stable vegetable oil, such as sesame oil, sunflower oil, or wheat germ oil, and you can easily compose your own body oil, or why not pimp your fragrance-free organic body lotion with your favorite scent? Essential oils are available in well-stocked health shops.

Find the right essential oil

HOW DO YOU WANT TO FEEL RIGHT NOW? PICK YOUR OIL TO FIT YOUR NEED!

REVITALIZING: lemon, bergamot, peppermint, mint, and rosemary.

CALMING: ylang ylang, lavender, mandarin, jasmine, and bergamot.

WARMING: ginger, cinnamon, and blood orange.

SENSUAL: rose, cedar wood, and patchouli.

COOLING: eucalyptus.

Vegetable oils for different needs

Body oils and various cosmetic creams are most often based on a vegetable oil. There are plenty of vegetable oils to choose from, and it is better to pick a product with vegetable oil than artificial mineral oils that do not nurture the skin at all, but stay there like a film. Natural oils all have different beneficial effects, so be sure to read the list of ingredients to see which oil suits your skin type and what it is in need of right now.

Reduce wrinkles!

ARGAN OIL – is a thin oil that penetrates the skin quickly, containing vitamin E, carotene, triterpenes, and phytosterols. It keeps well, is nourishing and makes fine wrinkles less visible. It is said to be good for damaged, aged, and sensitive skin, and to have a calming anti-inflammatory effect.

For dry and aging skin!

AVOCADO OIL – is extracted from the flesh of the avocado and is moisturizing, mild, and very fat which makes it suitable for dry and aging skin. The oil keeps well and contains lecithin, carotene, vitamin D, vitamin E, and pantothenic acid. It can easily be used together with an essential oil.

Anti-inflammatory!

HAWTHORN OIL – is rich in vitamins A, C, and E, as well as protein, beta carotene, and saturated fats. Quickly absorbed by the skin, the oil also contains various antioxidants and is said to have anti-inflammatory qualities, to prevent aging, to make skin more elastic and glowing, to be good for eczema, and to soothe sunburns.

For oily skin!

JOJOBA OIL – contains almost exclusively mono-unsaturated fats and provides a natural sunscreen of factor four. It is an emollient that can perfectly well be used on hair and as nail oil and cuticle oil. Its composition is similar to that of the skin so that it does not clog the pores and therefore it is suitable for people with oily skin.

Soothes sunburns!

COCONUT OIL – is made from the flesh of the coconut and contains mostly saturated fatty acids. In Asia it is frequently used both in cooking and on the body. The oil is solid in temperatures below 77F. It's good for dry skin and brittle hair, and has a soothing effect on sensitive skin, as after sunburn. It is also said to be effective against various types of fungi.

> **BEWARE!**
> Always test new skin care products gently into your elbow where the skin is thin and see that it goes well and that you tolerate the product.
> Even natural ingredients can cause allergic reactions.

Suitable for massage oil!

OLIVE OIL – contains for the large part mono-unsaturated fat, anti-inflammatory polyphenols, chlorophyll, vitamin E, and antioxidants. It is perfect as massage oil and is very effective on dry and cracked skin.

Natural sunscreen!

SESAME OIL – is to Asia what olive oil is to the Mediterranean—it is used for everything! The oil contains equal parts mono- and poly-unsaturated fats and loads of natural antioxidants. It is a natural sunscreen with a factor between two and four. It softens and protects and is said to aid healing.

It is used in oil pulling, or oil swishing, a traditional folk remedy mentioned in the Ayurvedic texts of India.

Soothe skin irritations!

ALMOND OIL – for best effect use pure cold-pressed almond oil. It is mild and softens and soothes skin irritations. It keeps well, contains a medium amount of fat, and is mainly composed of mono-unsaturated fats. Almond oil is excellent as a massage oil as it is not absorbed immediately by the skin. It works well for removing make-up, styling hair, and reducing fine wrinkles.

Natural protection

Mooncup is a silicone menstrual cup designed by woman to be a convienient, safe, and eco-friendly alternative to tampons and sanitary pads. Mooncup offers an end to the waste, discomfort, and expense of disposable sanitary protection. It is made from soft medical grade silicone, the Mooncup is latex-free and contains no dyes, BPA, toxins, or bleaches. On average, one woman will use over 11,000 tampons or pads in her lifetime, which will end up in landfill or in the sea. One woman uses up to 22 items of sanitary protection every period. Regardless of your flow, you only need one Mooncup, and it lasts for years and years, making it the most economical sanitary product you can buy.

Let your smile change the world—but don't let the world change your smile.

Add rose petals in a little water and you get a simple rose water which has a refreshing effect on the skin.

Store vegetable oils in a dark and cool place, preferably in a tinted bottle. Sunlight makes the oil turn rancid faster.

Cut a beetroot and use it as rouge.

Mix organic raw sugar with sesame oil and you get a nice body scrub.

DIY skincare products

Facial bliss

Oil boost

1 tsp sesame oil
1 tsp olive oil
3 drops essential rose oil

Stir together in a small bowl. Pat into slightly damp skin. Rose is a luxurious essential oil appreciated by mature skin.

Fruit boost

1 ripe avocado
2 tbsp natural yogurt
1 tsp honey

Mash the fruit and mix in the yogurt and honey. Massage into skin. Leave for 10 minutes and then rinse off with warm water.

Oat mask

Oats and honey have anti-inflammatory properties.
½ cup rolled oats
¼ cup water
2 tbsp honey
Fresh squeezed lemon juice

Grind rolled oat flakes in a mortar or run in mixer until powdery. Mix in remaining ingredients and stir until smooth. Apply on face, and leave for 20 minutes. Rinse off with warm water.

TIP!
Store vegetable oils in a dark and cool place, preferably in a tinted bottle. Sunlight makes the oil turn rancid faster.

TIP!
If you have dilated capillaries and veins or varicose veins, apply wheat germ oil.

Body bliss

Body rub

3 tbsp organic sugar (if you want a finer scrub for the face use icing sugar)
1 tbsp sesame oil

Mix together and massage your skin wearing silk gloves, so called kese bath gloves, preferably every morning.

Oats and lavender scrub

½ cup rolled oats
5 tbsp water
2 tbsp vegetable oil
5 drops essential oil of lavender

Run the oats in a mixer until powdery. Mix in water and oils. Massage with circular movements onto arms and legs. Rinse off with lukewarm water.

Body oil

½ cup vegetable oil (olive, almond, or sesame)
20 drops essential oil

Pour the oil into a dark glass bottle, add the essential oil. Choose the oil according to what effect you want. See Essential oils on *page 77*. Close and shake the bottle. This body oil will keep for at least a year if kept in a dark place at room temperature. Apply on slightly damp body for quicker absorption.

Soft hands

Unscented organic liquid soap
½ lemon
Organic hand cream or organic olive oil
Cotton gloves

Pour water into a small bowl. Add a little mild, organic, unscented soap and squeeze in lemon juice. Now you have good water for washing your hands, just soak them for 10 minutes. Dry your hands with a soft towel and slather on the cream or the olive oil. Put on the gloves and go to sleep. Your hands will get thoroughly moisturized overnight.

Bath for a weary body

To take a bath with herbs is really beneficial for body and mind. If you don't have a bath tub you can use a foot bath or a hand basin. For best effect make an infusion of the herbs first. An infusion is similar to a tea, but stronger and more concentrated. For a bath you need about 7 ounces of fresh herbs that you put in a big bucket. Pour in a bucket of boiling water and let it steep for about twenty minutes. Pour the infusion into the bath tub. When you make an ordinary infusion the herbs are strained off, but you can keep them in for the bath. Top up the bath tub with water, as hot as you can stand, but do be careful if you have high blood pressure. Soak for 15–20 minutes in the tub, then air dry and dress in warm clothes and rest for a while.

Source: Gröna apoteket, Norstedts

Bath salt

1 cup Himalayan salt
2 tbsp dried lavender or roses

Mix the ingredients. Sprinkle a couple of tablespoons in lukewarm water. Enjoy! Keep the salt in a glass jar with lid.

Bath bliss

1 large grapefruit
1 cup organic coconut milk
2 tbsp honey
15 cardamon seeds

Squeeze the juice of the grapefruit into a bowl. Add coconut milk and honey. Pour into a warm bath together with the whole cardamon seeds.

Happy feet

3 tbsp flake salt
Sesame oil

Put warm water into a clean basin. Stir in the salt. Let your feet rest in the bath as long as it feels good. The salt invigorates and extracts deep lying dirt. Massage the feet with warming sesame oil afterwards.

Dental care

Ordinary toothpaste contains substances that are harmful to health and environment, such as parabens, Triclosan, and sodium lauryl sulphate.

There is, however, an alternative to commercial toothpaste which is easy to make at home. For the children's sake, make sure they brush with gentle toothpaste.

Naturally white teeth

Baking soda has been used as toothpaste for many generations. It is a gentle polish with anti-bacterial properties. It is one of the basic ingredients in most homemade toothpaste recipes.

Popular essential oil flavours are peppermint or wintergreen, but do try cloves, anise, or tea tree oil. The latter is also antiseptic.

Sparkling White

- Brush with baking soda, sea salt, or anise powder a couple of times a month.
- Chew licorice root and scrub your teeth with the frayed bits.
- Rub the teeth with salvia or basil leaves.

Toothpaste

½ cup baking soda
10 drops essential peppermint oil
Water
Bowl
Sea salt
3–6 tsp coconut oil

Put baking soda in a bowl, and add the essential oil. Add water in small amounts while stirring until you have a smooth paste. For a more gel-like texture, try adding 3–6 tsp coconut oil. Mix well and store in a covered container.

Healthier hair

It is definitely worth changing a shampoo with its synthetic components for an organic alternative; it's better for both the environment and your hair. Most common shampoos contain sulphates to make it lather. Sulphates are dehydrating and do not break down easily in nature.

Silicone is also a common ingredient in conventional shampoos. It coats each hair with a film, making the hair seem soft, smooth, and shiny. When you change to homemade shampoo, be patient; it takes a while for the body to eliminate all the toxins.

Another alternative to freshen your hair is to use a dry shampoo. It soaks up grease and makes it easy to style. Apply it close to the scalp.

Remember that the more toothpaste and shampoo lathers and foams, the more chemicals it contains.

Dry shampoo

2 tbsp potato starch or corn starch

Sprinkle as close to the scalp as possible, using a tea strainer. Brush off superfluous powder.

Hair pack

Rhassoul clay, from Morocco
2 tbsp coconut oil
Big outer leaf of cabbage
Towel
Rubber band

Water down the clay and smear it onto the scalp. Squeeze in the coconut oil only on the tips of the hair. If your hair is long twist it up on top of the head.
Put the cabbage leaf on your head, like a helmet; secure it with the rubber band. Keep it on for at least half an hour. Then wash your hair as usual with an organic shampoo.

Split ends

2 tbsp olive oil
2 tbsp sesame or castor oil
1 egg
1 tbsp coconut milk
1 tbsp liquid honey

Mix the ingredients with a hand blender. Spread the mixture on the hair and leave for fifteen minutes. Rinse off with lukewarm water.

Make-up

Rouge

1 beet root

Cut the beetroot in half. Using one half, rub it from cheek bone up towards the hair line.

Shelf life

To make creams and skincare products last as long as possible, various synthetic preservatives are used. There are, however, natural ways to preserve products, such as adding organic alcohol made from organic grains. Essential oils also have some preservative effect and will prevent mold from forming for a while.

Bright eyes!

2 tea bags, camomile
Water

Boil the water and pour into a bowl. Add the tea bags and let steep five minutes. Take out the tea bags; let the water drain off and place in the fridge until cool. Put a tea bag on each eye and leave for 15–20 minutes. Turn them over after half the time. You can use warm bags, but the cold decreases the swelling better and is more soothing. It is the tannin in the tea that diminishes swelling, as it is astringent and anti-bacterial.

Useful aids

In the bathroom and for skin care we need cotton balls, wipes, wash cloths, and pads. There are good ecological alternatives on the market. The most eco-friendly thing you can do is investing in an organic wash cloth that you can wash and reuse. You can also crochet your own wipes, see below.

For make-up implements choose those made of wood. Keep brushes, sponges, and other things fresh; rinse off regularly with warm water and organic soap to prevent dirt and infection-causing bacteria from building up.

TIP!
When you make your own creams, make enough of a batch and store in tinted jars and bottles with tight lids so they keep longer.

Knit your own wash cloths, too. Just knit them three times the size, or any size you prefer.

Eco-smart wipes

Choose an organic cotton yarn in a color you like. Cast on 12 stitches on size 6 needles. Knit all rows until cloth measures about 2 inches. Cast off and secure the ends. When they get dirty put them in a mesh bag and wash in hot water in washing machine.

Buy organic

Aubrey – *aubrey-organics.com*

Ahavaus – *ahavaus.com*

Bentley Organic – *bentleyorganic.com*

Body Shop – *thebodyshop-usa.com*

Burt´s bees – *global.burtsbees.com*

Dr Bronner – *drbronner.com*

Dr Hauschka – *drhauschka.com*

Eminence Organics – *eminenceorganics.com*

EO Products – *eoproducts.com*

Green People – *greenpeople.com*

John Masters Organics – *johnmasters.com*

Jurlique – *jurlique.com*

Lagona – *logona.us*

Living Nature – *livingnature.com*

Lush – *lush.com*

M.A.C – *maccosmetics.com*

Nature's Gate – *natures-gate.com*

Neals Yard Remedies – *us.nyrorganic.com*

Niko Cosmetics – *niko.com*

Origins – *origins.com*

Primavera – *primaveralife.com*

Suki skincare – *sukiskincare.com*

Upper Canada Soap – *uppercanadasoap.com*

Weleda – *weleda.com*

Shop green on Internet

Many of the brands in the list have their own web stores!

CHECK THESE, TOO:

theremustbeabetterway.co.uk
mountainroseherbs.com
skinactives.com
saffronrouge.com

❗ SEVEN CHALLENGES:

1. Make your own facial bliss with ingredients from your own pantry such as oats and honey.

2. Try not to use deodorant for a month, rather change what you are eating and you won't smell bad.

3. Clean out the bathroom cupboard. Check the 'Best Before Date' and throw out everything that is old. Same goes for your make-up bag.

4. Exchange your usual facial mask for your own, using avocado and yogurt perhaps.

5. Try oiling your body; add an essential oil to suit your mood for the day.

6. Invite your friends to an organic spa day and make your own creams, bath salts and oils. Blend, test, and taste.

7. Wash your hair at most twice a week and you will notice how your hair will regain its natural shine and even curls.

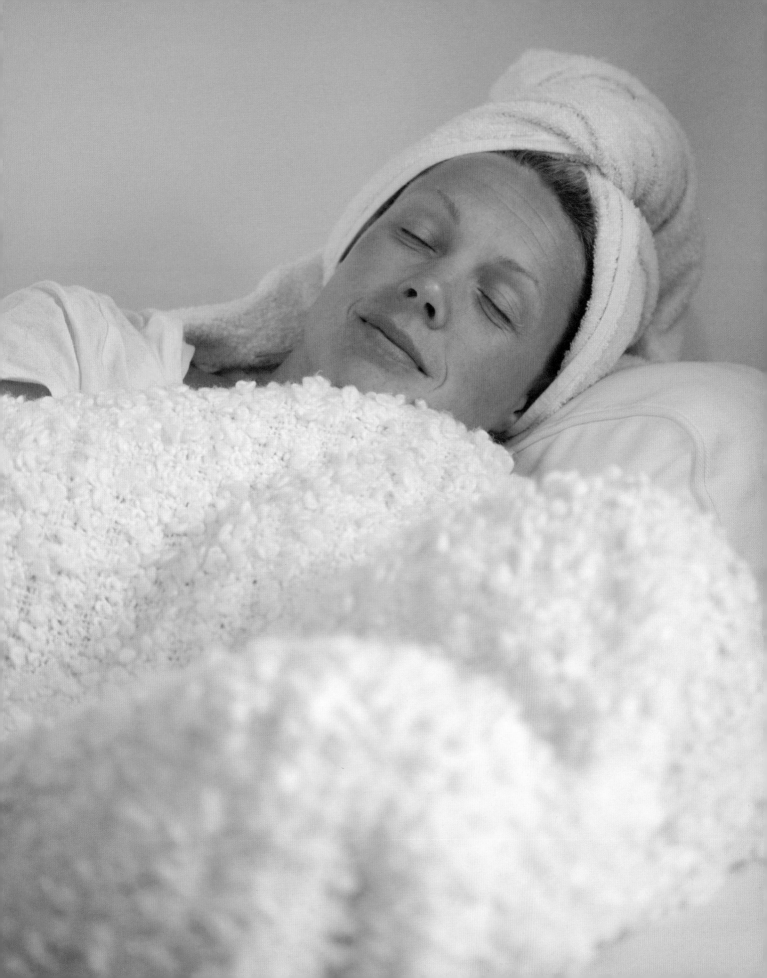

CHAPTER 4

THE GARDEN

HOW TO FARM ANYWHERE

In retrospect

About 100 years ago agriculture went from the small scale to the large where the latter uses fertilizers and biocides to increase the crop yields, albeit quality was lost in the shuffle. Conventional cultivation show clearly how the soils leach minerals, and decrease nutrient levels.

To make plants even more resistant to disease and pests they are now genetically manipulated in order to withstand all the biocides to which they are exposed. We have now seen that weeds have become resistant to herbicides which means new herbicides will need to be developed. We have no idea of how these new concoctions will affect nature.

In many greenhouses plants grow with only a nutrient solution and never see the sun. Fruit is picked unripe and travels long distances before reaching the consumer.

Conventional, or chemical cultivation, uses inorganic nutrients and biocides, like herbicides, fungicides and pesticides, hormones, and GMOs. GMO is short for Genetically Modified Organisms. A GMO may be a plant, an animal, or a micro-organism that has had its genes altered by man in an artificial way which cannot happen naturally or by ordinary plant breeding, such as cross-pollination or hybridization. GMO means that you can, on the molecular level, transfer genes from one species to another, or alter a single gene governing a specific trait. Soy, canola, corn, and cotton are among the crops that are genetically modified in many parts of the world, if not organically grown.

Many are convinced that GMOs threaten biological diversity. The pollen of GMO crops may spread to both cultivated and wild plants of similar species, threatening organic farming.

Biotechnology companies have developed GMO crops and these companies have patented plants and animals. The farmer becomes dependent on a few multinational corporations.

Plants are fed by adding nutrients directly to the plant which leads to an imbalance in the micro-organisms in the soil. Imbalance leads in turn to pest infestations and more pesticides are applied. The toxins harm the micro-organisms and more toxins are used. It has become a vicious circle.

Ever more soil is destroyed in this way. Close to 30 percent of all arable soils are depleted. Soils have lost 80–90 percent of their minerals in 70 years. Conventional farming emits four times more phosphorous and nitrogen than organic farming. As an example, 40 percent of Denmark's groundwater contains the herbicide Roundup (*source: www.monsanto.no*). This in turn leads to sick animals and people, which causes a lot of suffering in both.

Each individual has to take a stand in this matter. How do we want the world to look in 70 years? How do we want to feed ourselves—with toxins or natural crops from a healthy and happy earth? The choice is ours!

Plant where you live!

Do you live in...

... an apartment or a condo?

– Plant on a small scale in old PET bottles and hang in the window. Sprout or plant in pots, see *page 105*.

... an apartment with a balcony?

– A mini-greenhouse is perfect for the balcony. Pots work well, too. Use your own compost soil or buy eco-soil. Keep in mind that your plants need watering each or every other day. Spices, herbs, berries, greens, and exotic fruit can easily be grown on a balcony.

Remember that plants with large root systems, like tomatoes and potatoes, require much more soil and large pots, from 1 to 1.5 feet deep, while herbs, strawberries, and radishes can manage in 4 to 6 inches.

- Potted soil dries out faster than that in the garden, so be sure to water.
- Choose pots with draining holes, or drill them yourself, so excess water can drain off and not drown the plant.
- After 3–4 weeks the nutrients in the soil are used up. Fertilize with water-soluble plant feed according to specifications. Ordinary plant feed works well.
- If you live on a street with heavy traffic, just shower the leaves if they get dirty, and the plant will be healthier and tastier!

... a house with a garden?

Grow your own vegetables! Make the most of the harvest from fruit trees and berry bushes.

Soil

Good soil is teeming with life. It's alive with bacteria, fungi, dew worms, and other useful little critters—about 2 lbs of them in each cubic yard of soil! They live by breaking down organic material, withered flowers in the compost, leaves on the ground, or a dead hare in the forest, to the end products of carbon dioxide and water. In the process nutrients are released and various organic combinations (humus) are formed. For the soil organisms to be able to deliver nourishment to the plants they need constant feeding—like compost, garden waste, grass cuttings, and bark mulch. Then they restore a reserve of nutrients in the soil that the roots use as needed.

"We have to practise awareness of each thing we do, if we want to save our Mother Earth, and ourselves and our children as well. For example, when we look into our garbage, we can see lettuce, cucumbers, tomatoes and flowers. When we throw a banana peel into the garbage, we are aware that it is a banana peel that we are throwing out and that it will be transformed into a flower or a vegetable soon. This is exactly the practise of meditation. When we throw a plastic bag into the garbage, we know that is is different from a banana peel. It will take a long time to become a flower. Throwing a plastic bag into the garbage, I know I am throwing a plastic bag into the garbage. That awareness alone helps us to protect the Earth, make peace and take care of life in the present moment and in the future. If we are aware, naturally we will try to use fewer plastic bags. This is an act of peace, a basic peace action."

– Thich Nhat Hanh

Compost

Compost soil is the best soil! It gives our plants a soil full of nutrients, enriches the ground, making heavy soil lighter and light soil heavier. It reduces biocides that may come with the soil we buy.

If your community has a Solid Waste Program, follow their recommendations. If you have a garden you can put most of your garden waste into it, but avoid noxious weeds and invasive species. Kitchen scraps, like vegetable matter, tea bags, used coffee filters, and eggshells are good, but no cooked food, meat, or fish leftovers as they attract rats, racoons, and even larger animals like bears.

For millions of years nature has developed an amazing system for all living organisms. Everything hangs together in one huge ecological system, where all parts depend on each other— SYMBIOSIS. We humans, and the animals, live in this eco-system and have to do so without causing too much damage. Nature is balanced if we do not disrupt its ability to nourish what is growing. Wild plants have optimal nutrients and biophotons.* When we cultivate and add manure, the natural process is diminished. When we then take a step further and add chemicals to the plants, we ruin the whole symbiosis. Modern agriculture with chemical fertilizers is only about 150 years old. GMOs and irradiated produce appeared only 15 years ago. It is a relatively short time, but during this short time modern agriculture has caused Nature and Mother Earth substantial harm.

*Biophotons, or ultra weak photon emissions of biological systems, are weak electromagnetic waves in the optical range of the spectrum—in other words: light. All living cells of plants, animals and human beings emit biophotons which cannot be seen by the naked eye, but can be measured by special equipment developed by German researchers.

Urban farming

Urban farming

Urban farming will become a necessity in the future. It is a way to reduce the vulnerability of city life and we need to utilize all available land in the larger cities for cultivating. We are facing a crisis of resources with energy shortages, while at the same time the global economy is teetering. The food chain is fragile, and if one link fails we go without food.

Even if urban farms can not make cities completely self-sufficient, they are still an important contribution, not least for the mind. A pallet collar with carrots in the middle of town may make us stop and think about things like locally grown food, food production, and food security.

Food security

Food security is about guaranteeing people access to food and control of the production.

"Visions are better engines of change than threats, and real change begins at the local level." So says Björn Forsberg, author of *Time of Transition*, in which he describes several transition projects he has visited around the world.

In one of America's cities there are 65,000 abandoned houses and 46 percent unemployment after the automotive industry moved away—and with them many other companies, among them all the big grocery chains. Instead about 800 communal urban farms have sprouted, more than any other big city in the western world. Apart from producing food, urban farming also creates upward spirals by offering the unemployed something to do and improving the social climate. Some maintain that the urban farms have lessened violence and criminality.

In Havana, Cuba's capital with its 2.5 million inhabitants, 44,000 today work full-time in urban farming. In 2005 these farms produced 12 oz of vegetables per inhabitant each day. Compare that number to the recommended daily intake of vegetables which is 10 ½ oz.

Urban farming creates an ecological learning opportunity, where people, apart from farming, learn about nature's eco-system and its benefits, the importance of biodiversity, and about the city and politics. It makes people care more about environmental questions, which is important for the whole planet. It can also create greater understanding for the inconvenient, environmental political decisions that must be made.

TEN STEPS TO A PRODUCTIVE VEGETABLE GARDEN

1. *SELECT VARIETIES.* Vegetables don't thrive in just any place. Ask your local nursery which varieties are suitable for your area. There may be resistant varieties that can handle diseases in your area, or yield a better harvest in your climate zone.

2. *PLANT AT THE RIGHT TIME.* Normally it says on the seed envelope when to sow. In some regions the growing season is very short and you must time it precisely for an abundant harvest. In other regions you may be able to sow several times during the summer and have a longer harvest time. The best thing to do is to ask for advice at a local nursery or garden store.

3. *PREPARE THE SOIL PROPERLY BEFORE SOWING.* Use plenty of compost or fertilizer. If you don't already use fertilizer containing nitrogen, use one that does.

4. *SOW THE RIGHT WAY.* Sow the seeds at the depth and distance recommended on the seed envelope. Vegetables sown too close don't yield as much. It is better to spread them out. If you plant seedlings make sure they are not planted too deep, or they may rot. Make a hole just so the roots are covered.

5. *WATER PROPERLY.* Keep the soil evenly moist so the plants don't dry out, but don't water too much either. Water deeply and let the soil dry out a bit before watering again. Irregular watering will lessen the yield of most vegetables and may make cucumber and lettuce taste bitter. The best result is achieved by installing an irrigation system with a timer. Seeping hoses work well and will not soak the leaves.

6. *FERTILIZE REGULARLY.* Maintaining is important for almost all kinds of vegetables. Most of them need nitrogen every fourth to sixth week. Be careful not to overdo it though, as some veggies, especially tomatoes, will produce less.

7. *COMPOST.* A 3-inch-thick layer of organic matter covering the roots lessens the risk of weeds and helps to prevent drastic changes in the moisture content of the soil.

8. *WEEDS.* Weeds compete with the vegetables for the water, nutrients, and sunlight thus reducing the yield. Pull the weeds out by hand and hoe the soil often to keep the weeds in check as much as possible.

9. *HARVEST OFTEN.* Many vegetables and especially beans, squash, peppers, and cucumbers stop producing if you don't pick them often. Pick every second or third day. If you cannot eat everything you pick, share with friends and neighbors.

10. *KEEP PESTS AT BAY.* Many kinds of insects enjoy fresh vegetables as much as you do. Watch for damage caused by insects and protect your plants with pesticides made for vegetables.

To mow or not to mow, that is the question

Those of us who live in a house probably have a lawn in the backyard. It's great for kids and pets, but it needs mowing, weeding, and watering. Why not turn over the sod in half the lawn, or a quarter, or just a small corner? Dig it up!

One of the nicest and most rewarding ways of enjoying the garden is to grow your own vegetables. The gratefulness you feel as you harvest tomatoes, beans, and cucumbers for the day's meal is intensified by knowing you get the freshest, tastiest, and healthiest food Mother Nature can provide.

Growing vegetables is not very different from any other kind of gardening. There is however less room for mistakes. To succeed with veggies one must be consistent—to ensure that the growing conditions are maintained throughout the season. If the plants dry out even for a short period, or you forget to fertilize, a large portion of the harvest will be lost.

> *TIP!*
> *Make your own organic spray to fight aphids. Mix soap and water in a spray bottle.*

Slow gardening

Slow gardening is about having a dazzling garden or balcony—at a low cost and least possible effect on climate.

Slow gardening is part of the same philosophy as slow food. To let things take their time and to take pleasure in the fact that things do take time; in the home-grown flowers and vegetables, but also in watching them grow and blossom. It is simply the opposite of 'extreme makeover' and short-cuts. The message is simple: You do not buy a garden, you create it. You are working with nature, not against it. Slow gardening is about soil improvement, seeds and propagation, re-claiming, and recycling, how to harvest and compost, plan and select plants.

> *TIP!*
> **Read more in the book** *The Thrifty Gardener* **by Alys Fowler.**

Other ways of gardening

Lend your garden

If you don't have time or opportunity to garden, lend it to someone who has. It doesn't have to be the whole garden, but just a small part of it. How the agreement is formulated is up to the two of you. Perhaps you split the harvest? Perhaps the user will have access to the garden only at certain times so you and your family can enjoy it as usual?

Start a co-op

The more the merrier, and more people makes it much easier to start a garden. Start a co-op and share the tasks, the costs and, of course, the harvest.

Communal plots

If you have a green thumb and don't have a small plot, rent or borrow one.

Collect the windfalls

Have you got more fruit than you can handle? Share with others. Donate to the homeless, restaurants, day care, schools, or put out a basket by the sidewalk for others to enjoy. If you have time, try to use the fruit. It doesn't cost anything and you will enjoy the memories of summer and early fall all winter. Besides, the fruit is locally grown, organic, and has more nutrients than the fruit you would otherwise have to buy in the store.

You can freeze, preserve, dry, or cook fruit. Wrap each apple in newspaper and store in a cool place.

TIP!

Core apples and cut in rings. Hang the rings on a thin wooden rod. Pretty and tasty!

> *TIP! GARDENING APPS!*
> *Organic Gardening* **has a good Planting Planner**
> *Growing your own organic fruit*
> *Organic Gardening for beginners*
> **Book:** *Grow Your Food for Free . . . Well, Almost, by Dave Hamilton*

❗ SEVEN CHALLENGES:

1. Start planning how you could plant more where you live.

2. At harvest time check your area for what is available to pick. Even in a city there are often berries and leaves you can pick.

3. Grow edible flowers to decorate your food or put into ice cubes. Simple and pretty.

4. Buy a tomato plant; it works even in an apartment without a balcony, and you can enjoy your own tomatoes.

5. Ask your neighbor if he wants to garden together and split the harvest. You cut the work effort in half and it is more fun to share the joy when it starts to grow.

6. Make use of seasonal berries, fruit, and vegetables—jam, juice, dry, and freeze, and you will have food that reminds you of summer all year long.

7. Arrange your own little herb garden. Fresh herbs enhance food and can be grown in a garden, on a balcony, or in a window.

CHAPTER 5

WORK & PLAY
INCORPORATING SUSTAINABLE
LIVING INTO YOUR ROUTINE

Greener work places

Green routine

Green shopping

Green gifts

Make a contribution on vacation—volunteer!

Climate smart vacation

The green tourist

Travel slowly, experience more

SUGGESTIONS FOR THE WORK PLACE:

- Offer employees free fruit.
- Use only Fair Trade and organic tea and coffee.
- Encourage every employee to bring her own glass and mug to minimize washing up.
- Encourage employees to think twice before using the printer.
- Use recycled paper.
- If every employee uses her own towel instead of paper towels, it will help the environment.
- Instead of Christmas gifts and expensive Christmas dinners ask the company to donate that money to a charitable organization.

Greener work places

Many of us sit by the computer both at work and at home. Homo sapiens was not created to sit by a computer, but evolution has shown that humans actually adapt more and more to the conditions in which they find themselves.

So perhaps in a hundred years our bodies may look quite different. But today science is telling us to limit our computer time to four hours, and we should avoid sitting down in front of the TV or computer before bedtime. This is mainly because all that sitting makes us fatter and sicker.

IF YOU DO SIT BY THE COMPUTER A LOT, REMEMBER TO:

- Take mini-breaks, to lower stress levels and loosen muscles. Computers emit radiation that impacts the negative ions in the air. Too much of the positive ions will neutralize the negative ions, which may cause respiratory problems, tiredness, headaches, irritation, and digestive problems.
- Keep a rose quartz next to your computer and TV. The crystal helps protect you from harmful electromagnetic radiation (EMF).
- Keep green plants nearby for fresh air.
- Stand up and stretch every hour. If you have an adjustable workstation you can raise and lower, stand up and work twice an hour.
- Stretch your muscles several times a day.
- Lie down flat on your back on the floor twice a day to let your back rest. Three minutes is enough to restore your good posture.
- Drink water with a little lemon, lime, or fresh herbs to stay hydrated—making your mind and body feel better. Office environments are often dry and dusty.
- Go outside in daylight, even on rainy days. Eat your lunch on a park bench or take a quick walk around the block.

Green routine

- Reduce car travel. Walk or bicycle for short trips—these activities are good for your health as well as for the environment. Use the train or bus where possible.
- If you shop by car, do all the shopping in one trip per week and combine with as many other errands as possible.
- Carpool with other people.
- Use Park and Ride if available.
- If you take the car—driving slower (speeding along at 70 mph can gobble up 30 percent more gas than doing 55 mph) and accelerating gently uses less gas; drive smoothly!
- Try to go by public transport as often as possible.

TIP!
On riderecycle.com *you will find a bike made from reclaimed materials.*
If you drive, there are apps that show how to drive in a more environmentally friendly way.

Green shopping

Shopping can be a lot of fun—you feel prettier and fresher with a new dress, a bunch of flowers on the dining table, new cushions to match the seasons, or a cute sweater for your child.

No, you don't have to stop shopping, but do it with due consideration. Ask yourself, "Do I really need this gadget or this piece of clothing?"

- Buy organic and Fair Trade flowers
- Flea markets—both for buying and selling!
- Think quality rather than quantity.
- Try to find out as much as you can about the item you want to buy.
- Skip it and see if you can find something similar at home—you have more at home you can still use that you have forgotten, guaranteed!
- Bring cloth shopping bags when you shop.
- Run several errands at the same time if you drive.
- Buy candles made from real stearin, bees wax, or soy.
- If you cook—buy pots and pans that don't leach heavy metals. Invest in cast-iron pots and skillets that will last a lifetime with proper care.
- The brain reacts to impulses and impulse shopping usually leads to purchases that will soon become garbage. See if you can do an 'on approval' purchase or lay-away, then go home and think about it for a day. A smart move for both the environment and your wallet!

Old ladles get new life with some color and pattern.

Foot salt with lavender – mix Himalaya salt with dried lavender. Pour into a nice jar!

NELLYS
TRAILMIX
filled with
ENERGY

Whole cardamon seeds are as good in tea as in a lukewarm bath.

cardamon
for better
breath

Green gifts

Instead of buying presents, give something you yourself have really liked and used, and now may please a new owner. Why is it considered bad to give away something that has been very precious to us? Does everything have to be brand new?

- Cut off a pair of jeans to turn into a pair of shorts.
- Jazz up old T-shirts with textile paint.
- Make piggy-banks of glass jars.
- Make your own trail-mix from your favorite blend of nuts, seeds, dried fruit, and superfoods.
- Make your own face cream, see *page 81*.
- Make your own salt, herb salt, or a salt mix for the bath.
- Give away a book that had a message for you—a message you want to pass on. Pay it forward!
- Make flea market finds and decorate old ladles in your unique style.
- Knit a shawl or wash cloths and wipes, see *page 88*.

TIP!
Vintage Home: Stylish Ideas and Over 50 Projects from Furniture to Decorating, **by Sarah Moore.**

Junk Genius: Stylish Ways to Repurpose Everyday Objects, with Over 80 Projects and Ideas, **by Juliette Goggin and Stacy Sirk.**

Make a contribution on vacation—volunteer!

Combine pleasure with service and make a badly-needed contribution on your vacation. Rather than lazy lolling on a beach or hammock you can travel the world and save turtles, work on an organic farm, take care of horses, or help out at an orphanage. Check the web links for how you can make your vacation more eventful and interesting!

TIP!

Useful links:

globalvolunteers.org

globeaware.org

howstuffworks.com/economics/volunteer/information/volunteer-vacations.htm

wwoofinternational.org

Climate smart vacation

After working hard for a year, vacation is like a gift from heaven. Naturally you want to do fun things when you are free and a change of pace and place is wonderful. Just relaxing on a beach or exploring a new city is inspiring and recharges your batteries. But do we really have to travel every year? And does it have to be by air?

- Traveling by train is the most climate friendly form of travel. It may not be possible if the destination is many hundreds of miles away, then your vacation would be over by the time you get there.
- We don't have to stop flying altogether, but it is not sustainable to have us all fly long distances several times a year. Plan and pick a time when it is necessary to fly and in between choose a more climate-friendly mode of transportation. Flying charter is often better than regular flights as the planes are often full and are usually direct flights.
- Compared to taking a plane the car is not such a bad choice, especially an eco car. If you have the space, ask if your neighbor wants to come along and share the ride and minimize emissions.
- Bus is another alternative where many can travel with fewer emissions. You think perhaps that it will take too long, but make the journey a pleasure. Pack a picnic, a good book and, if the whole family is going, challenge each other in a parlor game.
- Choosing slower means of transportation is a good rule of thumb as there will be fewer emissions. If you go by boat, slow boats are not as bad as fast ones. High-speed ferries are not as eco-friendly as an ordinary ferry, as they emit more carbon dioxide.
- Instead of getting a hotel room, trade apartments or houses with someone who lives where you want to go. It is not only cheaper, but it also opens up opportunities to get closer to the culture and people you are visiting. The best thing is that you will perhaps go to places you had not expected to visit, or you will discover new places when you see that it is possible to swap your home for a home in a place you hadn't even dreamed of.

TIP!
Useful links to swap/lend your home:
homeexchange.com
lovehomeswap.com

The Green Tourist

Eco-tourism is a concept that is becoming more common. Eco-tourism is responsible travel to natural areas that conserve the environment and improves the well-being of local people.

Eco-tourism . . .

- minimizes harmful impacts in nature.
- is fun.
- does not destroy and wear down what you have come to experience.
- contributes to environmental and cultural awareness.
- benefits local populations and places economically.
- encourages exploration, curiosity, and respect.
- is an effective means of setting an economic value on conservation areas.
- creates employment and self-sufficiency in sparsely populated areas without harming the environment. It's a way to have your cake and eat it too.
- is a business idea of combining commercial tourism in a respectful and fruitful way with traditional economies and native cultures.
- is a form of tourism empowering natural and cultural preservation, with fewer environmental damages.
- is simply a more enjoyable form of travel for everyone involved—tourist, local population, travel agent, and, not least, Nature itself.

TIP!
Take the train rather than flying if possible.

Why eco-tourism?

Eco-tourism is a growing sector of the global tourist industry that contributes positively to the local environmental, social, cultural, and economic welfare around the world. Eco-tourism offers long-term solutions by preserving and improving the bio-cultural diversity and by protecting the natural and cultural heritage of the world. By increasing the potential for growth, eco-tourism is also an effective tool for local communities to fight poverty and achieve a sustainable development. Eco-tourism is also helpful in fostering a greener tourism on other fronts.

Vacation around the corner

A vacation on home turf can be a lot of fun. Dust off the bike and make excursions where you live. You will be sure to discover new and interesting places around the corner. Bring a picnic in a basket and it is easy to stop for a break and a bite.

BE CLIMATE SMART ON YOUR VACATION:

- "When in Rome, do as the Romans do!" Read up on and study the place before you go there. Be aware of local customs and laws; you are a guest in their country and expected to behave respectfully.
- Choose a smaller, locally-owned hotel rather than a multi-national hotel chain.
- Buy from the locals, organic and locally grown when possible and more of your money will stay in the country.
- Use water sparingly when you shower.
- Ask room service not to change towels every day; a couple of times a week is enough.
- Don't haggle for the sake of haggling. The pennies you save may make a huge difference to the seller.
- Don't buy items made from species threatened by extinction, like ivory and coral.
- Choose public transport or bike when getting around.
- Turn off lights and TVs when you leave the hotel room.
- Recycle plastic and paper on the spot.
- Avoid using the hair drier and let clothes dry by air.
- Bring a cloth bag when shopping instead of buying new plastic bags all the time.
- Ask the hotel to provide large water containers where you can refill your bottles. Bali is one country that has introduced this in their hotels, and their policy is that guests may question any hotel that does not provide water for the guests. All in order to minimize plastic waste.
- When you get home: report any shortcomings you noticed to your travel agent.

TIP!
If you fly, choose a non-stop flight to minimize take-offs and landings with their huge carbon dioxide emissions.

Travel slowly, experience more

Relaxation and harmony is what the big travel agencies usually advertise. But how relaxing is your trip if you have to visit all the tourist spots on the map? Slow Travel recommends the slow journey and is a new addition to the Slow movement.

In a world where we are constantly fed fast information and pushed to ever increasing speeds, the Slow movement, see more on *page 27*, is pulling the emergency brake and is moving against the current with firm steps.

They encourage a slower journey. In other words, stay in one place during the vacation instead of chasing the big tourist attractions from one hotel to the next. Even the travel to and from the destination could be slower.

Nicky Gardner, editor of *Hidden Europe* is a genuine Slow Travel promoter *www.hiddeneurope.co.uk*

She believes a rushed trip destroys the contact with the surroundings while a leisurely travel restores it. The main idea is not to be in a rush, but to allow oneself to be open to a place for a longer time so as to get a greater and deeper appreciation for an area.

NICKY'S BEST SUGGESTION FOR SLOW TRAVEL:

- Enjoy the café culture! Sit down and do some people watching.
- Eat and shop locally and do what the locals do; don't just go by the guide books.
- Learn a few simple phrases and try out the language. Try to read the local newspaper with a dictionary at hand.
- Do not allow unexpected events to ruin your vacation, such as delayed trains or busses; it may open new paths you hadn't planned, leading to exciting adventures or interesting discoveries.
- The main idea behind Slow Travel is to be free to explore places at your own tempo and not to be tied to ought to's, so that you will feel better and make your trip more enjoyable and, above all, more relaxing.

❗ SEVEN CHALLENGES:

1. Check to see how you can make your work place greener.

2. Plan your next vacation and find out what kind of contribution you can make. Make yourself and others happy.

3. Think twice before taking the car. Is it possible to ride a bike, walk, or take public transport?

4. If you drive to work, ask your colleagues if you could share rides.

5. Would you like to swap homes during your vacation? What country do you dream about, and what are the alternatives?

6. Have a garage sale!

7. Next Christmas, make your own Christmas presents or give away something you have used and liked very much, for example: a favorite book, a potted flower, or the cardigan you never wear.

CHAPTER 6

ORGANIC FOOD AND RECIPES

RAW FOOD FOR YOU AND MOTHER EARTH

Raw food

Raw food is vegetables, fruit, roots, berries, sprouts, shoots, cold-pressed oils, honey, algae, fermented veggies, certain cereals, and superfoods. The ingredients are not heated above 107F to preserve nutrients, live enzymes, and biophotons as much as possible.

The food is prepared by blending or in a food processor. Some of the following recipes will require a de-hydrator.

The de-hydrator 'oven' is set on low temperature for several hours to dry the food; it is still climate smart as the temperature is so low and you can dry large amounts of food at the same time.

Raw Food Ingredients:

- Green leaves, vegetables, and roots
- Wild edible leaves
- Fruit and berries
- Nuts: pecans, walnuts, Brazil nuts, cashews, filberts (hazelnuts), and almonds (even though it is a stone fruit)
- Seeds: chia seeds, sunflower seeds, pumpkin seeds, hemp seeds, and flaxseeds
- Fermented foods: kimchi, kombucha, coconut kefir
- Oils: olive oil, coconut oil, hemp oil, flaxseed oil, almond oil, and pumpkin seed oil.
- Algae: hijiki, arame, nori, wakame
- Sweeteners: honey, agave, stevia, coconut palm sugar, fresh dates, raisins, cranberries, dried figs, and apricots
- Superfoods: (food with maximum of nourishment per ounce, included in these recipes): camu-camu, raw cocoa powder, raw cocoa nibs, goji berries, acai, lucuma powder, carob powder, cocoa butter

Our natural choice of natural food

Raw food is one of the most climate smart and eco-friendly ways to eat; it's good for the earth and for us.

All you need to prepare raw salads are your own energy and imagination.

It is not about eating a 100 percent raw food diet to make a difference, but to start thinking along a more raw and organic direction when you do your grocery shopping.

Food is flown around the world.

It may have come from the other side of the world, yet it is said to be fresh. To keep it as fresh as possible in transport requires a lot of fuel. The shelf life of perishable produce is prolonged by biocides and refrigeration, which keeps it from ripening.

SHOP HERE

- Farmers market.
- Have your organic box delivered each week.
- Find supermarkets with an organic selection.
- Grow your own!

The Industrialization of food

Do you really know what the food on your plate contains? When you choose organic foods and make your food from scratch, you need not keep track of weird E-numbers, be fooled by euphemisms such as "natural coloring agents," which are far from natural, or flavorings concocted in a laboratory to resemble the taste of, for instance, strawberries.

Our sense of taste, which we have used since time immemorial to determine if the food is edible, is now tricked by all additives so we can not discern the genuine tastes.

Candy is colored to look like berries. Berries in particular are something we are pre-programmed to eat in order to get the benefit of the antioxidants, so the candy makers are very clever in using these tricks to get us to eat more of their candy.

Many in the western world today do not have time to either become aware of their food purchases or to cook from scratch, with the result that many are actually suffering from malnutrition and yet are overweight due to poor eating habits and not enough exercise.

We eat and eat, but the food we eat has only empty calories with no nutrition. Our cells are screaming for more nourishment. The food we eat is 'stressed'; it has been produced through gene manipulation and is over-fertilized, and this is transferred to those of us who eat this food.

How is the food on your plate doing?

During the last decade we have learned that cattle is crowded into ever smaller areas and given hormones, and genetically modified to grow faster and bigger. The dairy industry is far removed from the cow grazing in the meadow and milked once a day by careful hands. Today the cow is pregnant again and again, and the calf spends very little time with its mother before it is removed so that we can get the milk. They are milked so hard their teats become sore and infected, for which they are then given antibiotics. There are 80 different types of antibiotics allowed in the dairy industry—drugs that are transferred to us who drink the milk.

Chicken and poultry live in crowded cages stacked on top of each other and do not see daylight during their lifetime. Their feed makes them grow so fast that their bones can't keep up.

Fish is scooped out of our oceans and many species are facing extinction. Those who are raised in fish farms are fed low quality feed. The vast food industry shuns no methods to make as much profit as possible.

Eating for body and soul

The more food is processed, heated, and frozen, the less nourishment it has. Availability of food and its so-called shelf life, making it look good on the store shelf, is more important than its nutritional value.

Food must be digested and broken down, as part of the eco-system. If it does not, then we can be sure it has been sprayed and contains chemicals to delay this process. We are better off eating as clean and unprocessed food as possible. Food is essential for living; it is not just something we pop into our mouths, but part of something much greater. Raw foodstuffs are alive with very much the same biochemical building blocks as ours. Food is energy but food has also a spiritual dimension. How it grew or how it was raised, handled, stored, and prepared plays a big part in what kind of energy it transfers to us. We eat not only to feed the body, but also the soul.

Try to become aware of how you choose your food. If the cow was happy, then its meat will be better, too. If the fish swam wild, it had better nourishment than the farmed fish. To be able to pick the better alternative we keep an eye open for organic products with the Fair Trade label. This tells us that the animals have been treated right and you lessen the risk of hormones and other chemicals entering your mouth.

With a raw food vegan diet we can nourish 36 more people than with the 'usual diet.' The distribution of our resources is skewed; no one should have to go hungry in this world.

Choose organic!

Do you want to eat something somebody else has sprayed with toxins? We don't believe in what we can't see. When we eat organic food, grown in nutrient-rich soil that has not been depleted by synthetic fertilizers and exhausted by too intensive use, then we allow ourselves the best nourishment. How can poor soil produce the nutrients we need? Yes, the chemicals in conventionally produced food do affect us. Why else would non-organic banana plantation workers die at an average age of 34? Wouldn't their health be worth a little higher price?

It is not yet known how all these chemicals affect us, as it is still a relatively new phenomenon, but many children with ADHD and autism have been seen to improve when eating clean organic food.

We will never be completely free from the chemicals, or we would have to stop breathing and drinking. We absorb toxins in many different ways. What we can do, is to make the choice to lower the risk.

If it is not possible for you to make organic choices in everything, take a look at this list and start by exchanging those products which are most affected by chemicals.

TIP!
Making an organic choice is a simple way of protecting our planet.

Organic food is cheaper

It takes a lot of work to get money for food. Why not work a little less and perhaps use that time in making your own food? In the chapter about Growing food, *page 97*, you can read about growing food if you live in an apartment. Organic food has more nutrients, so you don't have to buy as much food. Choose quality over quantity, it pays!

When you have a different relationship with food, you will adjust your shopping better and be more mindful of wasting it. It is a lot of money that ends up in the garbage every year.

ORGANIC FOOD ...

- has more nutrients per ounce.
- tastes much better.
- is not genetically modified (GMO).
- has ¼ less emissions.
- makes for healthier people and animals.
- uses less of finite resources such as oil, phosphor, etc.
- binds more carbon dioxide to the soil.
- does not harm the soil—creates sustainable farming.
- promotes healthy and natural cycles.
- prevents soil depletion and protects soil nutrients.

YOUR FOOD WILL ALSO BE FREE FROM:

- Herbicides
- Pesticides
- Fungicides
- Fumigants
- Nitrates
- Additives
- Preservatives
- Antibiotics
- Irradiation
- GMOs
- Toxic metals

Did you know that ...

... 12 percent of our wages are spent on food?
... 40 percent of the food we buy has empty calories?

BUY THESE ORGANIC:	OK IF NOT ORGANIC:
Apples	Onions
Celery	Sweet corn
Sweet bell peppers	Pineapples
Peaches	Avocadoes
Strawberries	Cabbage
Nectarines	Snow peas
Grapes	Asparagus
Spinach	Mangoes
Cucumbers	Eggplants
Blueberries	Kiwis
Potatoes	Cantaloupes
Kale/greens	Sweet potatoes
Green beans	Grapefruit
	Watermelons
	Mushrooms

Source: ewg.com

Avoid these—and feel better

The movies Hungry for a Change *and* Food Matters *by James Colquhoun and Laureintine ten Bosch, have opened our eyes to how the food and pharmaceutical industries work. Below are some of the food additives they write about on their web site www.foodmatters.tv*

Food additives have been used for centuries to enhance the appearance and flavor of food and prolong shelf life. But do these food additives really "add" any value to your food?

Food additives find their way into our foods to help ease processing, packaging, and storage. But how do we know what food additives are in that box of macaroni and cheese, and why does it have such a long shelf life?

A typical American household spends about 90 percent of their food budget on processed foods, and in doing so are exposed to a plethora of artificial food additives, many of which can have dire consequences to your health.

SOME FOOD ADDITIVES ARE WORSE THAN OTHERS. HERE IS A LIST OF THE TOP FOOD ADDITIVES TO AVOID:

ARTIFICIAL SWEETENERS – found in diet or sugar-free sodas, kool-aid, ice tea, jelly (and other gelatines), desserts, puddings, drink mixes, baked goods, cereal, sugar-free gum, breath mints, chewable vitamins, and toothpaste.

HIGH FRUCTOSE CORN SYRUP – found in most processed foods, bread, candy, flavored yogurt, salad dressings, canned vegetables, and cereals.

MONOSODIUM GLUTAMATE (MSG / E621) – found in Chinese food, many snacks, chips, cookies, seasonings, most Campbell soups, frozen dinners, and lunch meat.

TRANS FAT – found in margarine, chips, crackers, baked goods, and fast foods.

COMMON FOOD DYES (E133, E124, E110, E102) – found in candy, cereal, soft drinks, sports drinks, pet foods, fruit cocktail, maraschino cherries, cherry pie mix, ice cream, bakery products, American cheese, macaroni and cheese, carbonated beverages, lemonade, and more!

SODIUM SULPHITE (E221) – found in wine and dried fruit.

SODIUM NITRATE/SODIUM NITRITE – found in hot dogs, bacon, ham, luncheon meats, cured meats, corned beef, smoked fish, or any other type of processed meat.

BHA AND BHT (E320) – found in potato chips, gum, cereal, frozen sausages, enriched rice, lard, shortening, candy, and Jello.

SULPHUR DIOXIDE (E220) – found in beer, soft drinks, dried fruit, juices, cordials, wine, vinegar, and potato products.

POTASSIUM BROMATE – an additive used to increase volume in some white flour, bread, rolls. Potassium bromate is known to cause cancer in animals.

Remember to wash and peel non-organic vegetables and fruit.

If you choose raw, organic food you do not have to think about this long list—the food is FREE from all nasty food additives!

TIP!
- *Read the label to see where the food came from. Avoid those that traveled the farthest.*
- *Bring your own cloth bags.*
- *Buy refills when available.*
- *Buy Fair Trade products.*
- *Buy according to the season.*

Get started with Raw food!

To get started with Raw food you need a little time to establish a new habit. You need a blender and a food processor, lots of fruit and vegetables, nuts, seeds, and other yummy natural raw produce. Some ingredients may be new to you and you can read more about them in the list of ingredients on page 129.

What do you need in your raw food kitchen?

UTENSILS:

1. Knife and cutting board.
2. Blender – for milk, smoothies, creams, cheese cake fillings, nut/seed flour. Check which price range suits you and how often you will use your blender.
3. Food processor – for making nut/seed burgers or pie dough, when ingredients have to be chunkier, and when you make dough.
4. De-hydrator – is a special drying oven that can be set at 107F and has a timer. You can use an ordinary oven. Open the oven door now and then to let out the steam, or wedge the door to keep it slightly open.

Crunchy sprouts!

You can sprout all year round, no matter how small your place is. It is incredibly cheap and the yield is wonderfully nourishing and revitalizing:

- Climate smart – a few tablespoons of seeds/lentils will give you a plentiful harvest of sprouts with least harm to the earth.
- Nutrition – you get all essential amino acids, stuffed with chlorophyll. The nutritional value of that little seed increases by about 100 percent.
- Sprouting seeds/lentils/beans are about the cheapest food you can buy considering the nutrition you get.
- The shorter the time span between harvest and eating, the more nourishment and life energy you get when you make your own sprouts at home.
- When sprouts appear, put them in a sunny window during the day. The sprouts encapsulate the sunlight, making chlorophyll, which will benefit your body.

Add sprouts to smoothies, press the juice, put them on a sandwich, dry and use in snack balls, mix into a salad, or eat green lentil sprouts instead of chips and popcorn when watching TV.

SEEDS/LENTILS/BEANS TO SPROUT:
- Alfalfa seed
- Mung beans
- Green lentils
- Small lentils
- Chick peas
- Adzuki beans
- Fenugreek

HOW TO SPROUT:
- Use a large bowl, a deep pie dish, or a Mason jar.
- Cover: cheese cloth, newspaper, or a perforated lid.

PREPARATION:
1. Soak 1 tbsp seeds/beans in 2 cups of water for 4–8 hours. (Small seeds – shorter time, larger beans – longer time). Pour off the water and rinse carefully.
2. Spread the seeds in a pan, leaving a little water at the bottom.
3. Cover with cheese cloth or other, making sure it is not airtight, and place out of direct light.
4. Rinse with lukewarm water twice a day.
5. After 3–5 days (depending on seed you have chosen) the sprouts are ready.
6. Place in sunlight for a few hours to make them green.
7. Store the sprouts in the fridge and they will last at least 5 days.

You can also let your sprouts continue to grow into shoots or wheatgrass. Use planting trays or an old cookie tin, cover with soil, and sow your sprouted seeds. Cover or place out of direct light until little green shoots appear. Let stand in sunlight and water every day. After about 12 days you will have green shoots or wheatgrass.

MORE INFO:
The Sproutman Steve Meyerowitz *The Complete Guide to Sprouting*

Wild and Green

Wild greens are completely free and organic. During spring and summer buds are opening outside, the leaves are filled with sunshine and are bursting with energy. See page 165 for recipes for yummy smoothies made with wild greens!

EAT MORE GREENS!

- The chlorophyll in green leaves help cleanse the blood. It is said that the cleaner the blood, the less risk we have for getting sick.
- Fresh green leaves contain about 70 percent fluid, just like us. That's why it is the perfect way to add fluids to our cells and avoid getting dehydrated.
- The green leaves are mineral-dense and contain good fatty acids and proteins. Everything for us to feel as healthy as possible!
- Green leaves are available whether we live in the city or in the country, just remember to avoid those growing along busy roads. I am grateful for the green leaves growing in our inner courtyard and I can get to them from our apartment and pick them. Easy and delicious!
- The wild leaves are locally grown and organic. Whatever there is in the air, soil, and rain we can not do anything about, but at least no one has sprayed them.

You can pick wild greens and dry them for winter and use them, for example, in teas, or to boost smoothies, in snack balls, or just sprinkle them over a salad.

They are free, ready to be picked. No one has intentionally planted this plant; it has grown wild and free, and spread all on its own and the seeds have found a spot to germinate and root, and grown up into a crisp green leaf. Mother Earth and Father Sky have cooperated: wind, rain, sun, and soil in synergy. When you eat wild green leaves you partake in the power, energy, and trust that everything is as it should be—you are filled with a vibrating life force. Wild green leaves vibrate at a very high frequency. Let your cells vibrate with those of nature!

Your amazing body

The human body is awesome, always wanting what's best for us. We, on the other hand, don't always give our bodies the best conditions.

Everything we eat, do, or don't do, such as no exercise or too little sleep, affects our bodies. We are always able to choose to stress our bodies less, and to provide more and better conditions for living longer.

Biological vs. chronological age

We could be of an age that is considerably older or younger than the age according to our passport. Our biological age is very much influenced by our lifestyle and starts to show around 40 years of age. That's when the aches and pains begin to make themselves known, if we have not taken care of ourselves. If we have been physically active and eaten mostly whole foods we are likely going to live longer.

HOW TO LIVE LONGER

- Eat until you are 80 percent full. (Studies have shown that mice fed a low calorie feed live 30 percent longer.)
- Eat high quality food.
- Drink 6 glasses of water a day, filtrated or spring water—see more on *page 147*.
- Move about for 30 minutes a day—better short and often than mega-exercise once a week. Remember the daily activity: take the stairs instead of the elevator, walk, or ride a bike to work or to the bus stop. Leave the car at home if you have to make a short errand.
- Try to get outdoors every day.
- Laugh a lot, have fun!
- Sleep at least 8 hours a night.
- Be aware of your unique potential in the universe as a whole.

Digestion—fight or flee

Stress affects our digestion more than we realize. The fact is that when we are stressed all our energy is prepared to flee. During stress the brain reacts as if we were being threatened and prepares the body to flee. When stressed all our energy is focused on eliminating the threat and there is no energy left to digest the food, which results in tummy aches. That's why it is so very important to relax and take a few deep breaths before each meal and to avoid stress during the meal.

Follow your gut feeling

Unfortunately the Standard American Diet (SAD) does not benefit the way your gut feels. To develop and sustain it you need to eat food full of fiber, free from gluten and lactose, which can irritate the intestinal lining; fermented foods and drinks are helpful. Our intestines need billions of bacteria to function as they should. Our intestines especially need fiber and we need to chew our food properly. 80 percent of our immune system's cells and many signal substances exist in the intestines. Your gut has a nervous system which is both complete and independent, and that's why our stomach is often called the 'second brain.' Read more about this in Michael Gerson's book *The Second Brain*. The stomach contains more nerve cells than the spinal cord, functions independently, and can cut off or ignore messages from the brain.

FOR THE BEST GUT FEELING!

- Eat probiotics or eat lots of fermented veggies, kefir, or kombucha.
- Eat food rich in fibers.
- Eat in peace to help digestion.
- If you need a lunch on-the-go, have a big, yummy smoothie.

You are sloshing!

Our bodies are 70 percent water and we must constantly make sure to keep that level. Today dehydration has become a disease as a result of drinking too much diuretic liquids such as coffee, tea, and soda pops.

We need to drink at least 8 cups of water a day, depending on whether we are men or women, and the season and activity level. When we eat fruit and greens we re-hydrate the body, but we still need to remember to drink water. It is almost unimaginable that we have so much water sloshing around inside. We need the water to send messages in the body; water acts like a carrier of nutrients, salt, and minerals.

Clean water

Tap water is unfortunately far from clean. It has passed through sewage treatment works where heavy metals, medications, and toxins have been filtered out. A water filter is a good investment; there are many variations from a simple jug to advanced systems. Choose one that works for you at home. If you live near a natural spring, go and fill up there with living crystal clear water with nature's own minerals intact.

Carbon filters remove chlorine, organic chemicals, volatile organic compounds, but not fluoride, trace metals, nitrates, or microbes; you need a more expensive and advanced filter. Up to 95 percent of the chemicals in your water can be removed with the help of a filter—which is good news!

Revitalize your water

When you filter your water you also remove some important minerals that exist naturally in spring water. You can add mineral drops and a pinch of sea salt and stir to replenish the water. Even berries, lemon, fresh herbs, or edible flowers will vitalize your water.

When water is forced into the pipes its natural movement is lost, too. To enliven your water you can buy a water whirler, or add a pinch of salt and stir the water with a wooden spoon, three times clockwise and three times counter-clockwise.

Water crystals

The Japanese scientist Masaru Emoto has researched our ability to influence the look of our water crystals. His hypothesis is that water crystals look different for different types of water. By sudden freezing he could see the crystals forming in different ways depending on what message the human being had given the water. Masaru wants to show how we can improve our well-being as the crystals form according to the energy we give the water. We are to a large degree made of water and when we say nice, kind words we form the water crystals into beautiful formations. The prettiest formations are formed by the words "Love and gratefulness."

Eating mindfully

Here is a quotation from the author Thich Nhat Hanh, a Buddhist monk who has spread the message of peace since childhood:

"A few years ago, I asked some children, 'What is the purpose of eating breakfast?' One boy replied, 'To get energy for the day.' Another boy said, 'The purpose of eating breakfast is to eat breakfast.' I think the second child is more correct. The purpose of eating is eating.

Eating a meal in mindfulness is an important practice. We turn off the TV, put down our newspaper, and work together for five or ten minutes, setting the table and finishing whatever has to be done. During these few minutes, we can be happy. When the food is on the table and everyone is seated, we practice breathing: "Breathing in, I calm my body. Breathing out, I smile," three times. We can recover ourselves completely after three breaths like this.

Then, we look at each person as we breathe in and out in order to be in touch with ourselves and everyone at the table. We don't need two hours to see another person. If we are really settled within ourselves, we only need to look for one or two seconds, and that is enough to see.

After breathing we smile. Sitting at the table with other people, we have the chance to offer an authentic smile of friendship and understanding. It is very easy, but not many people do it. To me it is the most important practice. We look at each person and smile at him or her. Breathing and smiling together is a very important practice.

After breathing and smiling, we look down at the food in a way that allows the food to become real. This food reveals our connection to the Earth. Each bite contains the life of the sun and the earth. The extent of how the food reveals itself depends on us. We can see and taste the whole universe in a piece of apple! Contemplating our food for a few seconds before eating and eating in mindfulness, can bring us much happiness."

> *TIP!*
> *Write beautiful, kind words on a piece of paper and attach to a water bottle, whisper these words to your water, or send words of gratitude next time you drink a glass of water. You fill the water you drink and yourself with beautiful crystals.*

❗ SEVEN CHALLENGES:

1. Start sprouting!

2. Try preparing a single raw food dish from scratch.

3. Exchange ordinary candy for raw food candy.

4. Drink one green smoothie a day.

5. Eat raw food for three days, or perhaps seven?

6. Take three deep breaths before dinner for a week. What is happening in your body?

7. Buy only organic ingredients for a month.

> *Read more about Raw Food in Erica's books about raw food and take a look at the inspiration list of raw food books:*
>
> - *Raw Food – The Complete Guide for Every Meal of the Day*
> - *Raw Desserts*
> - *Fabulous Raw Food – Your Way to a Lighter Life*
> - *The Green Smoothie Miracle*

YELLOW CAMU-CAMU LEMONADE

2 portions

In the morning it is important to re-hydrate your body and give it a gentle start. Before you eat a 'real' breakfast, start with a liquid to wake up the body. Camu-camu gives you a vitamin C boost!

3 cups water
2 tbsp honey
1 apple
1 tbsp turmeric
1 tbsp camu-camu powder

Mix all ingredients in blender and if needed, strain off pieces of apple.

Recipes

These raw food recipes will provide optimal nutrition, aid digestion, energize you from morning till night, and help you sleep better. The meals will provide vital water and if you choose organic ingredients, you will also avoid toxins getting into your food and body.

Raw food is designed by nature, not by man, to give you the vitality you deserve to have and the energy and stamina to change our world. Turn on your blender and enjoy the breakfasts, desserts, snacks, lunches/dinners, and smoothies! Yours is the power!

Breakfast

RAW FOOD MUSLI

About 10 portions

Musli is perfect for keeping on hand when you feel hungry between meals. During winter you can add millet, quinoa, or spelt flakes to make it more filling. If you want to stay 100 percent raw omit them. Make a big batch, while you are at it!

2 cups mixed nuts
2 cups mixed seeds
2 cups mixed flakes
2 cups mixed dried fruit

Run the nuts in the food processor at low speed until they are coarsely chopped. Place in a big jar or tin with a lid. Do the same with the seeds and dried fruit. Stir the flakes into the mixture. The musli will keep for a month or two in an airtight container.

RAW FRAPPÉ

2 portions

Frappé is a sweet coffee enjoyed cold in Greece. If you like coffee, use a little instant coffee; otherwise stick to a yummy chocolate milk or bambu coffee. Maybe raw frappé will become your new morning habit instead of café latte.

½ cup cashew nuts
1 ½ cup water
1 pinch vanilla powder or a splash of vanilla essence
1 tsp instant coffee—optional—or bambu coffee

1-2 tbsp raw cacao powder
1 tbsp agave syrup
2-3 ice cubes

Blend cashew nuts and water to a milk. Add the remaining ingredients and blend again. Taste and see if you want more of something. Serve with ice cubes.

SUPER GRANOLA

About 5 portions

Pep your breakfast with superfoods for best antioxidant boost!!

2 heaped cups buckwheat
½ cup flaxseeds
3 tbsp acai powder
¼ cup lucuma powder
1 tbsp vanilla powder

Soak the buckwheat for 4–8 hours. Rinse carefully. Leave to sprout for perhaps one more day. Soak flaxseeds in double the amount of water, let stand about 4 hours. Stir together buckwheat, flaxseeds, and the rest of the ingredients. Spread onto baking sheet and dry for 14 hours or so, dry until completely dried. Store in a jar with a lid.

MANGO SMOOTHIE WITH CASHEW

1–2 portions

Lassi is an Indian drink based on yogurt and usually some fruit. Frozen mango adds a delicious cool feel and the cashews make for a creamy smoothie.

1 cup cashew nuts
1 ½ to 2 cups of water
5 oz frozen mango
1 pinch of vanilla powder
2 dates—optional

Partially thaw the mango. Grind cashews until floury. Add 1 ¼ cup water. Blend again. Add mango and vanilla. Blend and taste. If you want it sweeter, add dates and more water if needed.

CHIA SEED PORRIDGE

2 portions

Breakfast, snack, or dessert—this porridge is made from mega-nutritious chia seeds and is good for any occasion. Chia seeds bind about ten times their own volume. The porridge needs to stand and swell at least 10 minutes, but will then keep up to 2 days. Very simple!

½ cup almonds
2 cups water
4 tbsp chia seeds

BUCKWHEAT WITH CACAO NIBS

2 portions

Buckwheat is good to eat during winter as it warms us from the inside.

1 cup buckwheat
1 cup almonds + 2 cups water (if you make your own almond milk)
2 tbsp hemp seeds, hulled
4 tbsp goji berries
4 tbsp cacao nibs
1 tbsp honey

Soak buckwheat 8 hours and rinse thoroughly. Blend almonds and water in blender. Pour the almond milk through a fine strainer or cheese cloth over a jug or bowl. You can also squeeze the milk through a fine sieve with a spoon. Mix buckwheat, hemp seeds, goji berries, and cacao nibs and serve in bowls. Drizzle honey over and add the almond milk.

Topping:
strawberry jam
thawed frozen strawberries
dried apricots, soaked 8 hours

Process the almonds to fine flour. Blend the flour with water to a milk. Strain through a nutmilk bag or fine sieve. Mix the almond milk with the chia seeds and allow to swell for 30 minutes. Stir. Mix strawberries with apricots to a smooth jam in a blender.

Serve the chia porridge with the jam.

Lunch/Dinner

KALE AND CRANBERRIES

2 portions

Kale in any shape is still a favorite. Try it as a snack, a side dish, or as a complete lunch!

6 kale leaves
a splash of lemon
a pinch of salt
½ tbsp olive oil
½ cup cranberries
½ cup walnuts

Shred the kale. Rub the kale with lemon, salt, and olive oil. Chop walnuts, add cranberries, and toss.

HORSERADISH DRESSING

4-6 portions portions

- to pour over fennel, pear, and cucumber. Yummmmmm!

½ cup cashew nuts
1 cup water
3 tbsp fresh, grated horseradish
juice of ½ lime
1 tbsp apple cider vinegar
1 tbsp olive oil

Blend the above ingredients to a smooth sauce.

BIG SALAD

About 3-4 portions

Make your own salad based on seasonal greens. Cut and decorate with the green sprigs of fennel, drizzle olive oil over, and voilá—your great meal is ready!

Green leaves
Turnip
Apple
Broccoli
Squash flower
Corn
Almonds
Green sprigs of fennel
Olive oil

Cut into thin slices:
2 pears
1 fennel bulb
1 cucumber

Serve with the dressing.

COOL GREEN PEA SOUP WITH MINER'S LETTUCE

2 portions

In spring and summer you can pick wild leaves to make a simple soup, that also work well for a smoothie. The frozen peas make for a cold soup, and the green leaves provide you with essential minerals your body needs to keep going.

2 large handfuls of miner's lettuce
1 handful of watercress
2–3 cups of water
1 pear
1/2 tbsp lime juice
1 avocado
2 cups frozen green peas

Mix miner's lettuce and watercress with water in blender. Add the pear, cut in large chunks, with lime juice and green peas, and blend. Add the avocado and perhaps more water and blend again.

KIMCHI BURGER

2 portions

Eating fermented vegetables every day strengthens your intestinal flora, which increases the ability to absorb nutrients in the food. Kimchi is a spicy variation.

½ cup almonds
½ cup sunflower seeds
2 small carrots
1 celery stalk
2 tbsp kimchi
a pinch of salt
juice of 1 lime

Chop almond and sunflower seeds finely in the food processor. Cut carrots and celery into smaller pieces and add kimchi, salt, and lime juice and process until all is well mixed. Shape into burger patties. Serve with a salad.

WALNUT BURGER

8–10 portions

Using a lettuce leaf instead of a burger bun makes this perfect for the picnic basket or lunch box. Decide if you wish to dehydrate them; they are still just as good!

1 cup pumpkin seeds
1 cup walnuts
7 sundried tomatoes
½ cup Portobello mushroom
1 ½ tbsp tamari
pinch of salt

red pepper
½ cup carrot
1 tsp paprika powder
1 tsp Italian spices
½ clove of garlic
1 tbsp olive oil

Turn the burger in ½ cup of pumpkin seed flour. Serve in a large lettuce leaf with a slice of tomato and an onion ring.

Cut the carrot in pieces. Run all the ingredients in the food processor until it is like dough, and shape into burger patties. Dry in dehydrating oven at 107F for 20 hours, turning over at half time, to give them a more 'cooked' feel. Will keep for 5 days in the fridge.

PAK CHOI

4 portions

Crispy cabbage is easily overlooked in the produce department, but is very good in a salad or softened in a dressing. You can also use bok choi in this recipe.

1 head pak choi
1 pear
10 snow pea pods
½ green pepper

Dressing:
¼ cup olive oil
1 ½ inch fresh ginger, grated
1 tbsp tamari
a smidgeon of coconut palm sugar
splash of apple cider vinegar
juice from ½ lime
¼ cup chopped mint
¼ cup basil
3 tbsp parsley
3 tbsp cilantro

Shred all vegetables finely. Toss together in a bowl. Chop the fresh herbs.

Mix the ingredients for the dressing and the fresh herbs. Fold in the shredded veggies and let stand an hour or so before serving.

BEETROOT AND ZUCCHINI NOODLES WITH MUSTARD SAUCE

2 portions

Root vegetables are easily eaten raw. With a spiralizer you can turn them into fun noodles!

2 beetroots
1 zucchini

Dressing:
1 cup cashews   *1–2 tbsp Dijon mustard*
½ to 1 cup water   *1 tsp vegetable bouillon/stock*

Peel beets and zucchini and cut into noodles using a spiralizer.

Grind cashews into flour. Add ½ cup of water and mix again. Add mustard and stock. Mix again. Taste, and add water or mustard if needed. Sprinkle with tamari seeds.

DEHYDRATED TAMARI SEEDS

Pep up your salad with dehydrated seeds or eat them as good snacks when you get hungry for something salty and delicious. Make a large batch while you are at it.

1 cup sunflower seeds
1 cup pumpkin seeds
1/4 cup tamari

Soak the seeds in 4–8 hours. Put the seeds in a bowl and pour tamari over the seeds. Spread out the seeds on a dehydrator tray and dry them for about 8-10 hours. Stir the seeds occasionally.

LASAGNA WITH CRISP CABBAGE SALAD

4 portions

For those who are a bit doubtful about un-heated food this Lasagna will give you a sense of "real food." The garlic cheese is very similar to melted cheese. To give it a bit of warmth and a feel of cooked food, heat the lasagna in the de-hydrator oven at 107F for 6 hours.

1 large zucchini or 2 small
1 large avocado or 2 small

Slice the zucchini with a potato peeler. Slice the avocado.

Garlic cheese:
1 1/4 cup macadamia nuts
2 garlic cloves
2 tbsp olive oil
a squirt of lemon juice
1/2 tsp salt

Chop the macadamia nuts coarsely in processor. Add garlic, oil, lemon, and salt and process until all is mixed.

Tomato sauce:
4 tomatoes
5 sundried tomatoes, soaked for 1 hour

Mix both kinds of tomatoes into a sauce in the blender.

Marinated mushrooms:
10 mushrooms
1 tbsp tamari

Slice the mushrooms, place the slices on a platter, and turn them over in the tamari. Let marinate for about 30 minutes.

Cover the bottom of a regular lasagna pan with zucchini slices. Spread half of the tomato sauce and half the mushrooms over the bottom layer of zucchini. Add one more layer of zucchini. Repeat and finish with a layer of zucchini, top with garlic cheese and avocado.

Cabbage salad:
4 portions
½ cabbage
1 tbsp cider vinegar
1 tbsp olive oil
fresh ground black pepper
a pinch of salt

Shred the cabbage. With your fingers rub the cabbage with cider vinegar, oil, and salt. Add black pepper. Serve with the lasagna.

FILLED ENDIVE LEAVES
5 leaves

Endives can be a little bitter and are nice for a change in a salad. The small leaves are perfect for finger food on a buffet.

4 wild mushrooms
4 cherry tomatoes
1 avocado
5 endive leaves
10 snow pea pods
3 tbsp watercress
2 small scallions

Marinade:
1 tsp tamari (1 tbsp if you use the less concentrated version)
½ tsp cider vinegar
1 tsp
juice from ½ lemon
5–10 drops tabasco

Cut the mushrooms into smaller pieces. Cut the tomatoes into quarters. Mash the avocado. Stir together the ingredients of the marinade and taste to see if you want more spicy tabasco or more salt with tamari. Fold the mushrooms into the marinade and let stand for 20 minutes or so.

Drain the mushrooms and add together with tomato pieces into the mashed avocado. Spoon the filling into the endive leaves and top with watercress and scallions cut into little rings. Serve with snow peas.

GARDEN BURGER

4 portions

Serve with a big green salad!

3 tbsp flaxseed ground in coffee grinder or mortar and pestle
6 tbsp water
½ cup celery
1 cup carrot
1 cup sunflower seeds
1 yellow onion
2 tbsp parsley
2–3 tbsp red pepper
3 tbsp tamari

Sour cream dressing:
1 ¼ cup cashews, soaked 8 hours
2 tbsp cider vinegar
2 tsp light miso
½ tsp salt
3 tbsp lemon juice
add water as needed

To serve:
lettuce leaves
tomato
avocado

Cut celery, onion, and parsley in small pieces. Grate the carrot and squeeze the juice through a strainer. Mix flaxseed and water in a bowl. Process sunflower seeds into fine flour and put in a bowl. Mix in tamari, parsley, vegetables, carrot and flaxseed. Shape into patties.

Blend all the ingredients for the dressing into smooth cream. Serve with salad, tomato, and avocado.

TOMATOES WITH OLIVE STUFFING

4 portions

4 big tomatoes
arugula leaves
1 ¼ cup sunflower seeds
5-7 sundried tomatoes, soaked (unless you use those in oil)
½ pot basil
½ cup black olives with pits

Scoop out tomatoes and put in a bowl. Rinse the arugula, place on a platter, and put the bowl with tomatoes on the arugula. Chop the sunflower seeds in the processor. Add sundried tomatoes, basil, and olives (pitted) and process. Fill the tomatoes with the mix and top off with a basil leaf.

RAW CARROT SOUP

4 portions

Soups are great and only take a few minutes. Serve with flaxseed crackers.

4 carrots
1 ¼ cashews
juice of 1 lime
1 red bell pepper
1-2 tsp tamari
¼ cup parsley
1 garlic clove
1 inch fresh ginger root
1-1 ½ cup water

Cut pepper and carrots into small pieces. Grind cashews finely in processor. Add lime, pepper, and tamari and process. Top with chopped parsley.

CHILI DIP

If you don't like it hot, omit the chili. Great for dipping cucumber slices and carrots!

¾ cashews
½ cup sundried tomatoes
1 red bell pepper
½ red chili pepper
3 tbsp olive oil

Cut bell pepper, sundried tomatoes and chili pepper (seeds removed) in smaller pieces. Grind cashews finely in processor. Add all together and process until creamy.

INDIAN BURGERS WITH PARSNIP RICE AND SPINACH SAUCE

4 portions

Creating raw variations of cooked food is always exciting. Here is one of my Indian burger variations, with spinach.

1 ¼ cashews
1 carrot
1 tsp turmeric
½ tsp chili powder
¼ tsp cayenne pepper
¾ inch fresh ginger root
juice from ½ lemon
pinch of salt

Cut the carrot in chunks. Chop cashews coarsely in processor. Add spices, salt, and ginger and process again. Add carrot and lemon juice and process until you can form mixture into patties.

Sauce:
1 ¼ cup spinach
1 ¼ cup water
1 avocado
juice from ½ lemon
1 tsp cumin
1 tsp turmeric
¾ inch fresh ginger root
2 tsp tamari

Blend all into a sauce.

Cabbage:
¼ head of cabbage or ½ a small head
juice from ¼ lemon
pinch of salt
1 tbsp olive oil

Shred cabbage finely. Add remaining ingredients and rub into cabbage until it softens, about 3 minutes.

PASTA SAUCE

2 portions

Serve with raw food zucchini pasta, carrot noodles, or just as a yummy tomato sauce. For extra strength choose garlic or chili pepper!

3 tomatoes
1 avocado
1 carrot
1 celery stalk
¼ cup sundried tomatoes
4 dates
red onion
2 tbsp olive oil
2 tbsp tamari/nama shoyu
2 tbsp fresh basil
1 clove of garlic
½ red chili pepper, seeds removed

Cut tomato, avocado, carrot, and celery into chunks. Run the tomatoes in the blender first and slowly add remaining ingredients. Go easy on the chili. Adjust to suit your taste buds.

Smoothies

OMEGA STRAWBERRY SHAKE

2 large portions

Hemp seeds are rich in omega-3 and contain protein that is easy for the body to absorb. The small shelled hemp seeds make the smoothie creamier.

¾ cup hemp seeds
2–2 ½ cup water
¼ tsp vanilla powder
4 dates
2 tbsp honey
15–20 fresh ripe strawberries

Mix in blender and add water until creamy.

PM Boost

1 portion

Mid-afternoon you may need an energy boost to keep going until dinner.

Acai powder has all essential amino acids and fatty acids and is chock-full of antioxidants

¾ cup almond milk
½ pear, ripe
1 tbsp acai powder
water to taste

Mix all ingredients in blender and pour into a tall smoothie glass. Serve with a straw.

TIP!
*Enhance your smoothies and your water with
pretty ice cubes. Pick edible flowers, like calen-
dula, clover, dandelion, nasturtium, and put in
each ice tray cube, fill with water and freeze.*

BLACK CURRANT LEAF SMOOTHIE, GREEN NETTLE SMOOTHIE,
AND GREEN DANDELION SMOOTHIE

COOL STRAWBERRY SMOOTHIE

2 portions

Like a milkshake but without milk, sugar, and nasty coloring agents.

2 cups almond milk (1/2 cup almonds soaked in 2 cups of water, or ready-made)
1 heaped cup strawberries
4 dates
1 handful ice cubes (omit if using frozen berries)

Blend almonds and water and strain off almonds in a fine meshed strainer or nutmilk bag. Blend strawberries and dates with the almond milk. If you use frozen berries you do not need to add ice.

GREEN NETTLE SMOOTHIE

2 portions

Nettles are one of the most nutritious greens. Pick the tender leaves for your smoothie.

2 handfuls of nettle
1 handful spinach
1 celery stalk
1–2 cups water
1 red apple
½ avocado
1 tbsp acai powder or blueberry powder
1 tbsp honey
a splash of lemon juice

First blend nettle, spinach, and celery with 1 cup of water. Add the apple and blend again. Add remaining ingredients and blend. Add water to your taste.

LAMBS QUARTERS WITH LUCUMA

2 portions

Wild greens are usually strong tasting, but are well suited for smoothies and salads.

3 handfuls lambs quarters
2 pears, ripe
4 celery stalks
1–2 tbsp lucuma
1–2 cups water

Blend ingredients with 1 cup of water. Add the rest of the water and blend to suit your taste.

GREEN DANDELION SMOOTHIE

2 portions

Dandelions are bitter. But the bitterness aids in digestion and gives the smoothie a maximum of chlorophyll.

1 handful dandelion leaves
2 handfuls green lettuce
1 cucumber
juice of 1 lime
1 avocado
1 tsp herbal salt
1–2 cups of water

Blend dandelions and lettuce with 1 cup of water. Cut cucumber in pieces and mix in. Add remaining ingredients and blend. If needed, add more water, depending on taste. Garnish with yellow dandelion flower and serve with flaxseed crackers.

BLACK CURRANT LEAF SMOOTHIE

2 portions

Use both leaves and berries from the black currant bush. You can also dry the leaves to make herb tea.

2 frozen bananas
1 handful black currant leaves
¾ cup black currants, thawed
1 ¼ cup water
4 fresh dates

Peel and cut the banana in pieces. Put in a freezer bag and freeze about 6 hours (or prepare beforehand and always keep frozen bananas on hand). Blend black currant leaves and berries with water. Add dates and bananas and blend to a creamy smoothie. If you have a powerful blender you can use less water and make the smoothie more like an ice cream.
Top with fresh black currants in season.

BLUEBERRIES IN GREEN

1 glass

Almond milk makes green smoothies more filling and creamier. It's good with apple juice, too—green and blue!

4 lettuce leaves
½ banana

½ cup frozen blueberries
½ cup apple juice
½ cup almond milk

Blend to a creamy smoothie

SMOOTH AND GREEN

1 glass

Smooth and gentle on the stomach with the creamy avocado, mango, and almond milk.

½ avocado
1 handful spinach
½ cup frozen mango
¾ cup almond milk

Blend to a creamy smoothie.

Snacks

AFTERNOON CRACKERS

10–15 pieces

Golden crackers with added coconut! Spread some coconut oil and top with a few fresh raspberries or raspberry jam made from blended raspberries and soaked apricots.

Preparation:
1 ¼ cup yellow flaxseed, soaked 4 hours in 1 ¼ cup water
¾ cup shredded coconut
3 tbsp coconut palm sugar

Run the soaked flaxseed and coconut in the processor to a batter like consistency. Add coconut palm sugar to taste and process again. Spread on cookie sheet covered with baking paper in a thin even layer. If you use a de-hydrator 'oven': after 5 hours place an empty cookie sheet over the crackers on the first cookie sheet and turn them over onto the second. Remove the paper and return to oven for another 5–10 hours. In a conventional oven turn the crackers over when you can lift them off the baking paper without sticking, and continue to dry until they are completely dry. Break into cracker-sized bits.

APRICOT CUBES

About 10

Only dried fruit have less fat and more of the healthy sweetness.

¾ cup fresh dates
¾ cup dried apricots, soaked 8 hours
2 tbsp coconut oil

2 tbsp cacao powder
¼ tsp vanilla powder

Process all ingredients to a soft mix in processor. Spread onto a plate and cut into cubes. Place in fridge for an hour or so before serving.

CHIA SQUARES

About 15

The sweetness from stevia, antioxidants from the chia seeds, and calcium from the sesame seeds make these squares perfect for a snack on the run.

¾ cup sesame seed
¼ cup almond oil
zest of 1 orange
¼ cup chia flour (or 3 tbsp chia seed ground to flour in coffee grinder)
2 tbsp carob powder
3 drops liquid stevia or tiny pinch of stevia powder
2 tbsp coconut oil

Blend sesame seed in blender or grind in coffee grinder, place in a bowl, and stir in almond oil. Wash the orange carefully and grate the peel finely. Stir the sesame seed and other ingredients together and put in a cool place before rolling into balls or squares—or put in a jar to have on hand when you are in a hurry.

LIME BALLS WITH COCONUT

10 balls

Coconut balls are a good alternative to other nuts, because they have healthy fats your body needs to function optimally.

zest of 2–3 limes
¾ cups fresh dates
½ cup shredded coconut
½ tsp vanilla powder

Wash the limes carefully and grate finely. Run ingredients in processor. If you need more liquid to bind the dough, use a little lime juice. Roll into balls.

INSTANT CACAO WITH BLUEBERRIES

2 portions

A snack that reminds you of a simple dessert, and does not take a lot of time to make.

¾ *cup thawed blueberries*
¼ *cup almonds, soaked 8 hours*
2 tbsp goji berries
2 tbsp cacao nibs

Chop the almonds and stir all ingredients together in a bowl.

SUN FRUIT SALAD

4 portions

Thawed blueberries make a fruit salad more juicy. A fruit salad is a perfect snack between meals.

10 strawberries
¼ *pineapple*
2 bananas
2 apples
1 cup blueberries
2 yellow kiwi
½ *cup cashews*
¼ *cup sunflower seeds*
¼ *cup pumpkin seeds*
¼ *cup dried cranberries*

Cut the fruit into smaller pieces. Mix all ingredients in a big bowl.

SHREDDED COCONUT AND ORANGE BALLS

About 10

These balls are for those who find nut balls are too filling.

¾ *cup dates, fresh or soaked*
½ *cup shredded coconut*
½ *tsp vanilla powder*
zest of 1 orange

Run in a small processor or double the batch. If you need more liquid, use orange juice.

NOUGAT BALLS

Desserts

MINTY BALLS WITH CACAO NIBS

About 10

Mint, chocolate, and creamy cashews! Delicious!

¾ cup cashews
1 tbsp honey
5 drops peppermint oil
2 tbsp cacao nibs

Chop cashews finely in processor. Add remaining ingredients and process until well mixed. Roll into balls.

NOUGAT BALLS

About 15

You can buy something called hazelnut paste, which I remember tasted very good. With that in mind, these balls came into being.

2 cups, slightly heaped, hazelnuts (filberts)
½ cup cacao butter
2 tbsp coconut oil

5 tbsp agave syrup
¼ cup carob
¼ tsp salt

Process hazelnuts into fine flour. Put cacao butter and coconut oil in a bowl over hot water to soften. Add cacao butter, coconut oil, agave syrup, and salt and process until well mixed. Add carob and mix again, and roll into balls. Place in fridge to cool before serving.

NUT CAKE WITH STAR ANISE, RASPBERRY FILLING, AND CAROB SAUCE

6 portions

The star anise lends a gentle taste of licorice that goes well with raspberry and carob.

Cake:
¾ cup almonds
½ cup sunflower seeds
5 dates
a pinch of salt
1 star anise

Process almonds and sunflower seeds to a fine flour, add remainder and process again. Press the dough into a glass dish or pan.

Filling:
1 lb frozen raspberries
1 tbsp coconut oil
1 tbsp honey

Blend all ingredients to a smooth cream. Spread over the cake bottom and place in fridge for about 30 minutes.

Carob sauce:
¼ cup carob
¼ cup water
3 tbsp coconut oil
2 tbsp agave

Blend all ingredients to a smooth sauce. Drizzle over the raspberry filling. Freeze until firm, about one hour.

MANGO SHERBET WITH CHOCOLATE SAUCE AND CACAO NIBS

About 2 portions

For a creamier texture add a frozen banana.

Chunks of 2 frozen mangos or 1 ¼ lb frozen mango pieces.

Sauce:
¼ cup coconut oil, warmed to a liquid
1 tbsp agave syrup
1 tbsp raw cacao powder

Topping:
2 tbsp cacao nibs

If you use a Vitamix you can use the frozen mango pieces directly by adding a tiny bit of water and blend. Otherwise, allow the mango to thaw a bit and mix with a little water in food processor to a sherbet-like texture. Serve in two bowls. Warm the coconut oil and stir in cacao powder and agave syrup. Pour over the mango sherbet. Top with cacao nibs.

BROWNIES

About 5 portions

1 ½ cups walnuts
¼ tsp sea salt
8 dates
1/3 cup carob powder or raw cacao powder
½ tsp vanilla powder
2 tsp water
1/3 cup dried cranberries

Chop ½ cup of walnuts and put aside. Process remaining walnuts, add dates, salt, carob, vanilla, salt, cranberries, and water. Spread a thick layer on a platter and sprinkle the chopped walnuts on top. Cut into squares.

ORANGE MARMALADE CRUMBLE-PIE

4 portions

Use the marmalade as a spread on a raw cracker.

1 ½ heaped cup of almonds
½ cup honey
2 tbsp canola oil
2 tbsp carob powder
1 tsp cinnamon
zest of 2 oranges
a pinch of salt

Filling:
3 oranges
10 dried apricots, soaked for at least 2 hours.

Process almonds finely, add carob powder, cinnamon, and salt and process again. Add remaining ingredients and process to a dough consistency. Press the dough into a pie dish. Blend oranges and apricots to a marmalade and fill the pie. Use a tea strainer to dust carob powder over the pie.

STRAWBERRY WHITE CHOCOLATE CHEESECAKE

16 pieces

How yummy can it get? A whole cheesecake free from gluten, lactose, and white sugar...

2 heaped cups pecans
8 dates
1 tsp vanilla powder
pinch of salt

Filling:
¾ cup cacao butter
3 cups cashews, soaked 2 hours
juice from ½ lemon
2 tbsp soy lecithin
1 tsp vanilla powder
½–¾ cup water
½ cup agave syrup
1 cup frozen strawberries, thawed
10 strawberries, thawed or fresh

Topping:
Fresh strawberries

STRAWBERRY WHITE CHOCOLATE CHEESECAKE

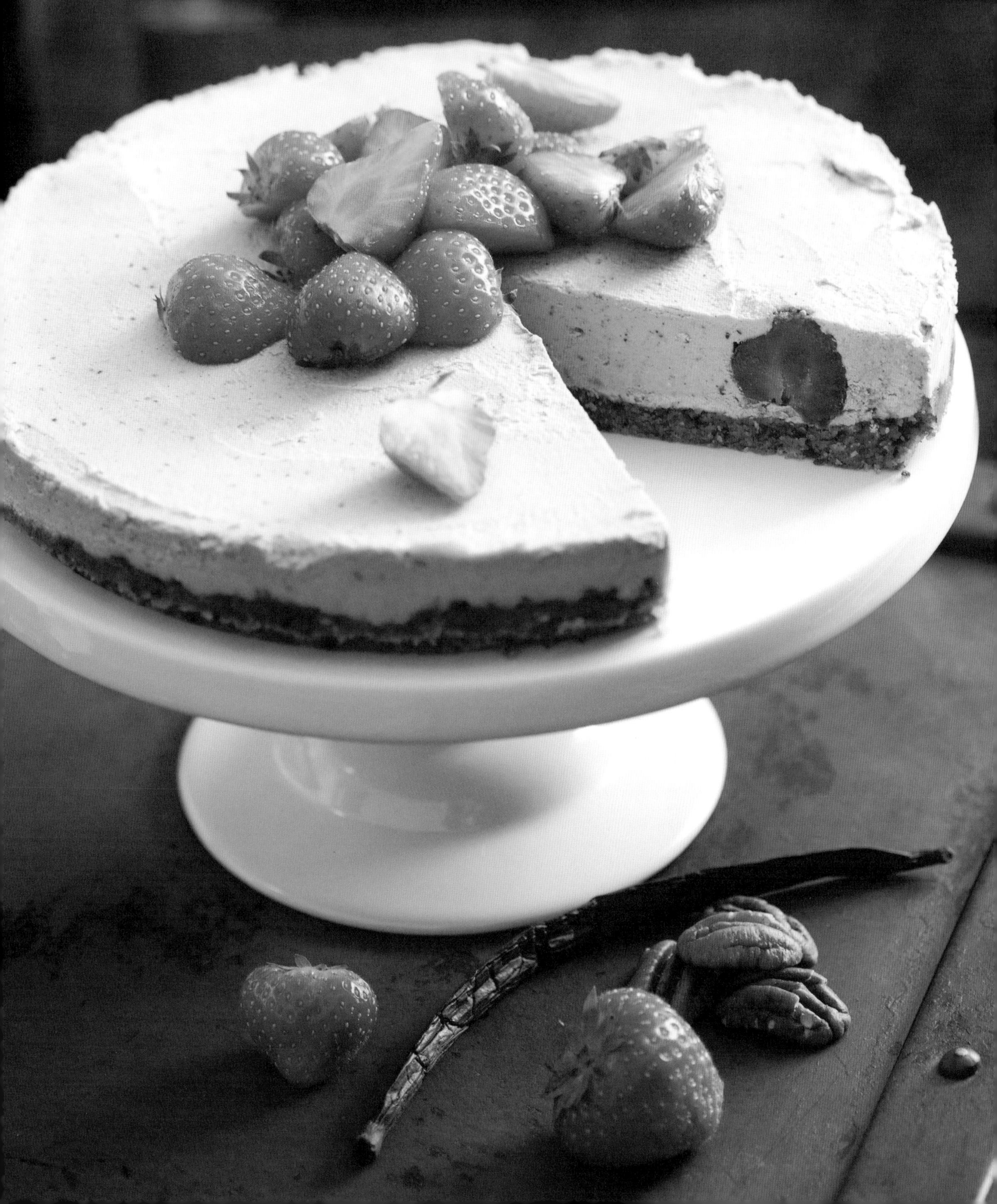

Grind pecans finely in processor. Add dates and run again. Add vanilla powder, salt, and process to dough texture. Press dough into bottom of spring cake pan. Liquefy cacao butter. Pour off the water in which the cashews soaked. Put the cashews in the processor with cacao butter, lemon juice, soy lecithin, vanilla powder, ¼ cup water, and agave syrup. Process until creamy. Add a little water if necessary. Put half of this cream into a bowl and set aside. Drain the melted juice of the thawed strawberries and add strawberries to the cream in the processor and mix. Pour the white cream over the pecan cake bottom and then pour the strawberry cream on top. Decorate the cheesecake with 10 strawberries and place in freezer for 6–8 hours. Thaw 20–30 minutes before serving. Add more fresh strawberries on top if desired.

RAW CINNAMON BUNS

About 30

With Raw Food you can still eat lukewarm cinnamon buns with a glass of cold almond milk. Oh, joy! You choose to serve them as is or 'baked' in the dehydrator/oven.

Dough:
1 ¼ cup almonds
¾ cup flaxseed, crushed
2 tbsp cinnamon
a pinch of salt
¼ tsp vanilla powder
2 tbsp coconut oil, liquid
2 tbsp water

Raisins for dough and filling:
20 dates
¼ and ¼ cup raisins, soaked 4 hours
1 tbsp + 1 tbsp cinnamon
½ cup sunflower seeds
2 tbsp water
½ tsp vanilla powder
½ cup water (use the water the raisins soaked in)

Dough:
Grind the almonds to fine flour in blender or processor. Crush flaxseed finely in coffee grinder. Mix almond flour, crushed flaxseed, cinnamon, salt, and vanilla powder in processor. Put dough in a bowl.

Process ¼ cup raisins, ¼ cup water, and ¼ tsp vanilla powder to a batter. Take half of this batter and add to the bowl with the dough, and mix. It may need 1–2 tbsp extra water. With your hands flatten the dough onto a cookie sheet covered with baking paper, about ¼ inch thick.

Continued . . .

RAW CINNAMON BUNS AND CLASSIC CHECKERBOARDS

Process the remaining batter with dates, ¼ cup raisins, 1 tbsp cinnamon, and sunflower seeds to a smooth batter. Spread onto middle of the dough and carefully roll it into a long roll with the help of the baking paper. Put in the fridge for about an hour before cutting the buns.

Cut into ½ to ¾ inch slices and let dry in dehydrator at 114F for 12–16 hours. Buns will keep for a week in the fridge.

CLASSIC CHECKERBOARDS

About 15

Swedes love little cookies of all kinds. I love to experiment and find raw alternatives that taste good and are good for the body.

2 ½ cup cashews
2 tbsp + 1 tbsp water
3 tbsp + 1 tbsp honey
a pinch of salt
3 tbsp raw cacao powder

Grind cashew nuts to fine flour in blender or processor. Add 1 tbsp water and 3 tbsp honey and process. Remove half the dough and put in a bowl. Add cacao powder, 1 tbsp water, and 1 tbsp honey and process the rest of the dough. Shape the two doughs into square sticks—2 white and 2 brown lengths. Line them up and squeeze together so they form a checker pattern when cut in slices. Place on cookie sheet. If you use a dehydrator put them on the checkered cookie sheet. Allow to dry for 8–12 hours. Will keep for 1 week in the fridge.

COCONUT MACAROONS

15–20

Macaroons are usually based on almond flour, but are given a touch of coconut here. You can decide if you want to use coconut flour or almond flour to vary the macaroons.

½ cup coconut flour
1 ¼ cup shredded coconut
zest of 2 lemons, about 2 tsp
3-4 tbsp lemon juice
¼–½ cup water
½ cup honey

Run coconut flour and shredded coconut in processor. Add lemon zest, lemon juice, and honey and process again. Add water gradually to taste and until you can form the dough with a spoon. Dry in dehydrator at 107F for 6–8 hours. They should be crispy on the outside and a bit dry inside, not doughy. Will keep for 2 weeks in the fridge.

COCONUT MACAROONS

LICORICE TRUFFLES

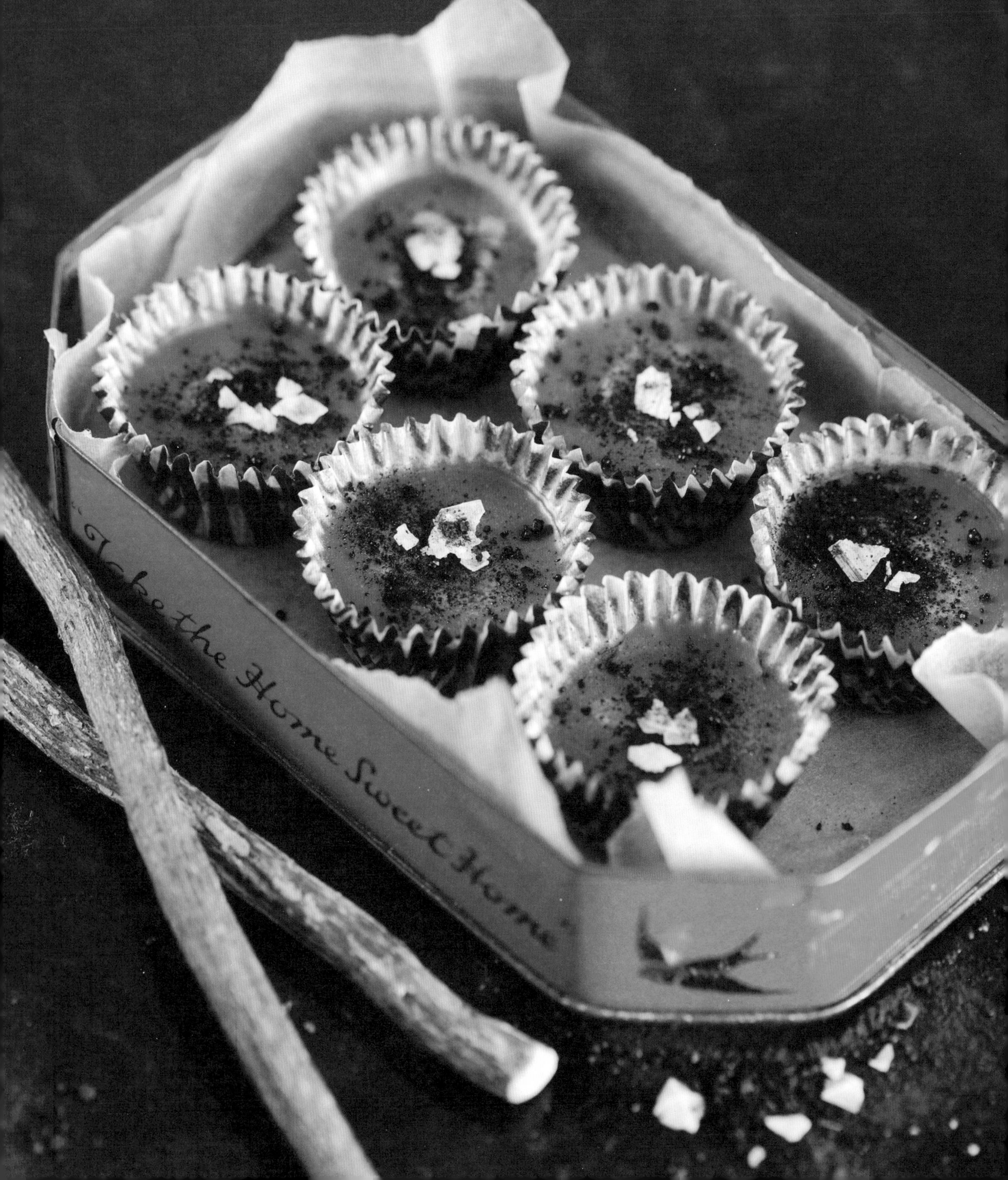

LICORICE TRUFFLES

About 20

Truffles flavoured with licorice powder will satisfy any licorice fiend. If you do not like licorice, try orange zest, peppermint drops, or lavender oil.

¾ cup cacao butter
½ cup coconut oil
1–2 tsp licorice powder
½ tsp raw cacao powder
1–2 tbsp carob powder
pinch stevia or 5 drops liquid stevia

Topping:
Flake salt and licorice powder

Liquefy coconut oil and cacao butter in bowl over warm water. Stir in the remaining ingredients, except for the flake salt, and pour into forms. Place in freezer for 2 hours. Let thaw 5–10 minutes before serving and top with flake salt.

STRAWBERRY CHEESECAKE WITH MARINATED STRAWBERRIES—LUXURIOUS!

6 portions

Naturally, marinated strawberries are great on their own if you can't prepare the whole cheesecake.

2 heaped cups cashew nuts
½ cup coconut oil, liquid
¼ cup honey
juice from ½ lemon
¾ cup frozen strawberries, thawed and with the melted juice

Grind cashews to a fine flour. Melt the coconut oil. Add remaining ingredients and try to mix without adding any more water. Works in a Vitamix, but ordinary blenders may require water. Pour the batter into a spring form pan. Freeze for about 6 hours. This cheesecake will keep for 2–3 months in the freezer, so make a few to have on hand.

Marinated strawberries
20 strawberries

Marinade:
juice and zest from 1 lime
2 tbsp coconut palm sugar
½ cup basil
2 tsp balsamic vinegar

ORANGE AND CHOCOLATE PASTRY

Slice the strawberries and place in a bowl. Chop the basil. Stir the ingredients for the marinade together and fold down the strawberries into it. Let stand for 1–2 hours.

Topping:
Sweet cacao nibs

Take the cheesecake out of the freezer 20–30 minutes before serving. Cover with the strawberries and top off with sweet cacao nibs.

ORANGE AND CHOCOLATE PASTRY

Makes 10

Orange and chocolate really complete each other. Enjoy a rich orange marmalade, crunchy cacao nibs and frosting. Each bite is an experience.

2 heaped cups walnuts
pinch of salt
12 dates
3 tbsp raw cacao powder
2 tbsp cacao nibs

Filling:
3 oranges
zest of 3 oranges
10 dried apricots, soaked 8 hours
2 tsp chia seeds

Chocolate layer:
½ cup coconut oil
3 tbsp raw cacao powder
3 tbsp agave syrup

Topping:
4 tbsp raw cacao nibs
orange zest

Process the walnuts fine, add salt and dates and process again. Add cacao powder and cacao nibs and process until dough can be pressed into a form.

Process oranges with the soaked apricots, orange zest, and chia seeds to a marmalade. Fill the forms with the marmalade. Liquefy the coconut oil and stir in the cacao powder and agave syrup and pour over the marmalade. Top with cacao nibs and place in fridge at least 15 minutes before serving, or put in freezer and let thaw 20–30 minutes. When the pastry is cold, you can remove the form.

CHAPTER 7

SPIRITUALITY

DISCOVERING THE FEELING OF TOGETHERNESS

Stay grounded

Mental gardening

Karma

Be a true believer

Inside and out

REALITY CHECK

In our daily obligations, commitments, activities, and energies from people we meet, we sometimes lose our own core. To find our way back we need to take a few minutes every day to check in with ourselves. Stop, feel where you are. Do nothing. Just sit and breathe. If possible, put your bare feet on the ground. After such a reality check we are better able to distance ourselves and not take things so personally, nor get too emotional, and the stress will ease off. It is also a good way to check where your energy level is that day. If you are tired—do less. Did you wake up on the wrong side? Let the day pass. Are you full of bubbling joy? Share it!

Stay grounded

In spring 2010 the book Earthing: The Most Important Health Discovery Ever? by Clint Ober, Dr Stephen Sinatra and Martin Zucker, was published.

It started a health revolution. It is a fantastic story of how Clint Ober discovered the health benefits of being grounded. It focuses on 12 years of Ober's research with some of the world's foremost researchers in biophysics, electro-physiology, and energy-medicine, and with doctors and sports researchers. It explains what happens when the body can assimilate the free electrons which eliminate the free radicals. A free radical is a molecule lacking one electron, which is thus is a weakened cell. When we are sick, our cells are damaged by free radicals. Today's air pollution means more free radicals than in earlier times. As the increased amount of free radicals affect our aging causing cell damage, we need antioxidants to help prevent this. Smoking, over-exertion, stress, medications, and processed foods also increase the amount of free radicals.

When we are in direct contact with the earth, we absorb the natural, subtle energy of the ground—the free electrons. With regular ground contact the electrons restore and stabilize the body's electrical state. Remember that our bodies—from cells to organs—function electrically.

The easiest form of grounding is to walk barefoot on grass, sand, soil, and rock, as humans have done from the beginning. To swim in lake and sea is another good way to get grounded. In our modern society we have insulated ourselves from contacting the earth's surface by wearing rubber-soled shoes outdoors, living our city-life on asphalt, walking on insulating wood or vinyl floors indoors, sleeping far from the ground, and spending almost all our time insulated from the earth.

LAW OF ATTRACTION

What do you attract into your life? What do you wish for? Can you sense that feeling already? Do you see your goal in front of you? Many say that the law of attraction works; that it is a law of the Universe. Whatever you wish to come to you, will come, if you truly want it and are open to this law working for you. The idea is to see the whole picture and not to worry about the details—it will all work out along the way. Aim for the goal and let the law of attraction do the rest. Unfortunately, the law of attraction has been a bit abused. It is not possible to be a couch potato in front of the TV all day and think that you will get the job of an executive, or a fit body. You must take action in the direction of your goal. Follow your inspirational gut-feeling, a feeling of ease, and things will work out.

Mental Gardening

We weed our gardens, clean our homes, do the dishes, but how often do we clean our minds of stuff we no longer need? Fear, negativity, worry, anxiety, and a stagnant mind—thoughts that are of no use to us are like mental dust-bunnies.

Grab a brush and soap and start scrubbing the nooks and crannies of your mind. You'll find a bit of worry here, a bit of fear there, and anxiety hiding in a pantry. Say bye-bye to these bits of debris and thank them for visiting, but that they are not needed anymore.

It is easier to think clearly when you have also cleaned out your body and you are feeding your body live, nutritious food that gives you energy and vitality. Start cultivating your seeds so they will bloom in your mind!

"Non Judgment Day" by Erica

One early, freezing cold morning I was out jogging when a thought struck me. A woman passed me with light and quick steps on an uphill path. I was huffing and puffing like an old lady and could hardly get up the hill. My thoughts began to spin: "Goodness, how I am puffing, why can't I run as smooth and easy, but am gasping up this hill with heavy feet?"

My whole system felt weak and I could not continue to run, and slowed to a walk. That's when it struck me that it was my own thoughts about myself that made me feel weak. I had judged and compared myself to someone else, instead of thinking I was actually pretty good, getting out of bed that bitter cold morning to go for a jog. The fact is that I have not been able to run for almost six years, as I have had spinal surgery resulting in daily pain. Nor have I prioritized exercising during Saga's infancy. That's when I began thinking that I need to pay attention to my thoughts and be aware of those judgmental and comparing thoughts when they popped up. I call it "Non Judgment Day." Since that day I have noticed them and look curiously at them, wondering if there is any truth in them. I accepted their turning up, and then released them. My "Non Judgment Day" continued and after a week I felt freer, lighter, stronger, and more at one with myself. These thoughts are intimately connected to raw food, in my experience. Those who say that someone eats better or worse than someone else, are really just comparing. But why do we have to compare?

We are on our own journey where we can discover, test, and experience what gives us greater joy and peace. For me, raw food has been and continues daily to be a beautiful tool to reach that place within myself.

Try to follow your heart, free from judgment and comparison. Try one, two, or three days to do a detox and a few "Non Judgment Days" and observe what happens within you.

Karma

In India and other Eastern traditions karma is something more than just superstition. The Indian caste system is based on karma. Whatever one believes about previous lives and the dissolution of karma, what is certain is that whatever we give comes back, like a boomerang. The Balinese approach is to improve karma by laughing and being happy.

Smile freely

To smile is one of the best things we can do. It doesn't cost anything, but spreads much happiness. Can you not smile? What is bothering you now that you cannot smile? Is it a worry about something that may happen in the future? We must let go of our worries about the future; we never know what will happen, so why waste all that energy on something that may not even happen?

When we smile, we release substances in our bodies that affect the whole system, our inner and outer healing. We look younger when we smile, too.

It is no effort to smile, it is the easiest thing we can do!

Smile and you will smile a thousand fold.

Be a true believer

Believe in your own transformation. Believe in the transformation of your neighbor. Believe in the transformation of the Earth. The day we stop believing something dies within us. It is faith, love and trust that carries us forward.

Dreams

Allow yourself to dream whatever dreams you want. What would you most of all like to do? Create your own dream world or dream map, and see which dreams are realistic and which may just remain dreams until time is ripe.

Many live totally shut off from their dreams. They do everything to distance themselves from finding that spark within, so it won't flare up to motivate them to move forward. Dreams are very precious and yet it doesn't cost anything to dream. They do take up your time, but it is time that is well spent, because you are actually doing something with the time that benefits you and gives you happiness and vitality.

Oneness/togetherness

We are all interdependent. It may seem nice to sit on a mountaintop and meditate all your life, to be enlightened, but interacting with our fellow beings, situations, and all kinds of weather is what life is all about. We are part of a whole, we belong together and we need each other.

It is said that if we have 3 minutes of eye contact every day with our family members, there would be no conflicts. To look into each others' eyes speaks more than a thousand words and we realize that we are only a reflection of each other. To meet someone's eyes for just a few minutes makes us feel noticed and rather vulnerable. Beautiful.

Try looking into your own eyes in a mirror for 3 minutes once a day for a week. Perhaps you see something you have never seen before: a unique, brilliant and fantastic person who exists just to make earth more beautiful.

How can we find a way to communicate with each other, understand our differences and benefit from them, rather than competing for everything? We all want to be loved, feel safe, to be seen, heard, and respected. Deep down we all want the same thing—peace.

Is someone you consider successful celebrated? Then let that person inspire you instead of putting him down and feeling you are not as good. We are all good, in different ways.

You got the whole world in your hand.

Inside and out

All life transformations need to come from the inside out. The only way out is in. Every change on Earth starts with the individual. The circumstances around a person are often just a reflection of what is happening inside.

We can only start with ourselves; we do not have to change the world. We need to change ourselves in order to change the world.

Peace on earth begins with peace within us. How can we promote peace if we are not at peace with ourselves?

Responsibility

We are born into this life with a responsibility, a responsibility we can not refuse. There is always something or someone else to blame, and if you want to find faults with something or someone it is easy. To free ourselves from blaming someone else and becoming a victim of circumstances, we can raise our own level and take responsibility for our part of the situation.

TIP!
Write down what angers you, or the thoughts you want to get rid of, on a piece of paper. Throw it out or burn it. You will feel both relieved and happy.

Do your best and leave the rest

Do your best. It is the only thing you can do. If you know that you have always done your best based on the conditions you have/had, you can stop worrying. Responsibility means always doing your best. For real. Your best is good enough.

Make your footprints smaller

How can we minimize the marks we leave on the earth after we die, or how can we compensate and add, so that we leave more than what we have taken? Perhaps this book will inspire you to take a few steps in a green direction? That in turn will result in fewer harmful footprints on the earth.

Upward spiral

A good choice leads to more good choices. We choose which spiral we want to be a part of: up or downward.

Do we want to share joy, trust, abundance, and laughter, or do we want to share fear, hatred, and dark thoughts?

What do you need to do in your life to move into the upward rather than the downward spiral?

When we start changing our eating habits to more organic and green food, it affects other parts of our life. If we start thinking about what we rub into our skin or what detergent we use, it will spread to other areas of our life. Like rings on the water, spreading ever farther in a positive spiral effect.

Cleaner food and cleaner Earth makes for a cleaner mind. Pure.

You are a rainbow

The chakra is an energy center, a link to the universal life energy. Each separate chakra has the task of receiving, regulating, and maintaining the physical, emotional, mental, and spiritual aspects of our health.

The aura is the energy field that surrounds all living things and can be seen as a band of light. You could say that the aura is a result of the energy we emit and is based in our thoughts, feelings, and body.

The chakra and the aura work in a symbiosis and the chakra is connected to various layers of the aura. Together they reflect the whole being that we are when acting in our environment and the universe as a whole.

Each chakra has a color related to vital functions. The root chakra, which is red, is at the base of the spine where we experience our security and foundation.

Just above this is the next energy center, which is orange and related to sexuality and creativity. The third chakra is yellow and has to do with personal power. The fourth, which is green, is the heart chakra through which we experience love. The fifth, blue, is found in the throat and deals with personal expression. The sixth, indigo, is in the forehead and is often called the Third Eye. It is the chakra of wisdom and has to do with our logical and intellectual capacity. The seventh chakra is at the top of our head and has to do with spirituality, healing, and transformation. Its task is to help us understand the spiritual aspect of life, and let spirituality become a part of us and be our guide. It is also the entrance for the life energy that flows through the whole physical body and the six lower chakras.

"We are like all the colors of the rainbow. You, as well as I."

❗ SEVEN CHALLENGES:

1. Check in with yourself one day this week. Stop and feel where you are, be aware of your breathing and each breath.

2. Smile at your own reflection in the mirror in the morning. Bring that smile with you all day. Smile at the bus driver, smile at the check-out girl in the supermarket, smile at your coworkers, and your children's teacher. They will smile back, guaranteed!

3. Get grounded. Stand by a tree, barefoot. Feel the ground under your feet and sense the link you have with the tree roots deep down in the ground.

4. Create your own dream land. What kind of work would you do? Where do you want to live? Where do you want to make a home? Write it down. Make a mood board where you pin up pictures that symbolize your dream life.

5. Did your coworkers get a pay raise, and you didn't? Did your neighbor win the lottery? Be happy for them instead of feeling left out. There is progress and happiness for us all.

6. Stop and pay attention every time you compare yourself to someone else. How does your body feel? If you look with joy at that other person instead—how does your body feel then? Not comparing yourself leads to more happiness in life.

7. Are you struggling with negative thoughts? Empty your mind. Tilt your head to the right and imagine your negative thoughts draining out of your right ear. Tilt your head to the left and imagine the rest of your negative thoughts dripping out of that ear. Tilt a bit in both directions and feel your head empty of destructive thoughts.

FLOW WITH GRACE

When easy is right. And right is easy.

Conclusion

The earth was born out of cosmos. It is one of many planets in the universe—an extraordinary and beautiful celestial body swimming amongst twinkling stars and an ever expanding galaxy, the Milky Way.

Our planet is unique in sustaining life. It is a living organism, an ecosystem from which plants, animals, and humans have evolved. We grew out of earth's womb. The earth is the Mother of Life, and we are her children. Sun, moon, and stars are our ancestors.

In the beginning every organism was independent, but eventually all started to cooperate and live together. Cells developed into living entities, each cell a little world of its own. Likewise the body became like a whole universe with its own world and galaxies.

Everything is interconnected and a perfection of the Whole.

The human being belongs to the cosmic body, and the universe resides within us. Our energy flows and cycles, influenced by the sun and the moon. We are indeed a part of a greater unity.

There is no inside and no outside. What occurs in the World is reflected within us.

The survival needs for Mother Earth are the same as ours. When we cause her harm, we also inflict it on ourselves.

Our body is part of the Earth's body. We breathe together, and whatever we discharge into the environment remains within us. We really don't have anywhere else to go.

All is one.

The world is our home, and this is where we belong.

– From a painting at Cas Bernats, Mallorca

Acknowledgments

We are grateful to:

- Our families for their support and love.
- Bianca Brandon-Cox for her calmness and kindness, for her amazing pictures and magical design of the book.
- Christel Palmcrantz Garrick who transformed our words to English and gave us wise advice.
- Our fellow man; we all inherited the power to be the change you wish to see in the world.

We do it together, one step at a time, filled with love for Mother Earth, Father Sky, and our divine spark.

Inspiration

Books:

100 sätt att leva ekologiskt; Mattias Henrikson, Helena Jansson, Ordalaget, 2010

Badskumt; Katarina Johansson, Ordfront, 2012

Gröna apoteket; Marie-Louise Eklöf, Norstedts, 2007

Handla rätt för en giftfri barndom; Anne Lagerqvist m fl, Lux, 2012

Lev enklare; Giséla Linde, Viva, 2008

Lisens indiska spa; Lisen Sundgren, Norstedts, 2010

Naturally gorgeous; Charlotte Vohtz, Ebury Press, 2007

Organic Home, Rosamond Richardson, Dorling Kindersley LImited, 2007

Omställningens tid; Björn Forsberg, Karneval förlag, 2012

Rainbow Green Live-Food Cuisine; Gabriel Cousens, North Atlantic Books, 2003

The Sunfood Diet for a Success System; David Wolfe, Maul Brothers Publishing, 2006

Wabi sabi, tidlös visdom; Agneta Nyholm Winqvist, Norstedts, 2011

The International Ecotourism Society, 1992

Websites:

alaeco.se, babyvarlden.se, choosingvoluntarysimplicity.com, ekoenkelt.wordpress.com, ekoturism.org, ecotourism.org, frokenekoreko.blogspot.se, framtidstigen.se, greenlivingideas.com greenlivingonline.com, greenlivingtips.com, hairmagazine.se, hallbarlivsstilwebbmagasin.com, hallbarturism.com, husmorsknep.se, livinggreen.se, naturskyddsforeningen.se, passionate-homemaking.com, shenet.se, slangintematen.se, slv.se, sustainabletourism.net, thedailygreen.com, travelcarecode.org, turkos.se, weleda.se, wlifestyleorganics.com, beeurban.se

For further inspiration about growing greens at Sky Horse Publishing:

Greens! Tips and Techniques for Growing Your Own Vegetables; Karin Eliasson

Frugavore, How to Grow Organic; Arabella Forge

Mini Farming Guide to Vegetable Gardening; Brett L. Markham

Window Gardening the Old-Fashioned Way; The Ultimate Self-Sufficiency Handbook

A Complete Guide to Baking, Crafts, Gardening, Preserving Your Harvest, Raising Animals, and More; Abigail R. GehringHenry T. Williams

Index